THE
GREEK
WORLD

Kingfisher Books, Grisewood & Dempsey Ltd
Elsley House, 24–30 Great Titchfield Street
London W1P 7AD

First published in 1987 by Kingfisher Books
10 9 8 7 6 5 4 3
Copyright © Grisewood & Dempsey Ltd 1987

British Library Cataloguing in Publication Data
Powell, Anton
The Greek World (Kingfisher History Library)
1. Greece — Civilization — Juvenile literature
I. Title
938 DF79

ISBN 0 86272 284 5 ✓

Edited by Anne Priestley
Designed by Nick Cannan
Picture research by Jackie Cookson
Phototypeset by Tradespools Ltd
Printed in Italy

The publishers wish to thank the following for
supplying photographs for this book:

12, 14 ZEFA; 15 Ekdotike Athenon S A; 16 *bottom*
John Decoupolis, *top* Ronald Sheridan; 17 *top*
Museum of Olympia, *bottom*, 18, 19 *top left* Ronald
Sheridan, 19 *top right* British Museum, *bottom right*
Antikenmuseum Staatliche Museen, Preussischer
Kulturbesitz, Berlin (West); 20, 22 Ekdotike Athenon
S A; 23 *bottom right* Ronald Sheridan, *bottom left*
Greek Tourist Office; 24 National Archaeological
Museum, Athens; 25 John Decoupolis; 31 *top left*
Ronald Sheridan, *bottom right* H.L. Pierce Fund,
Courtesy, Museum of Fine Arts, Boston; 32, 33
Michael Holford; 34 Ancient Corinth Museum; 39
Ronald Sheridan; 41 *top left* Ekdotike Athenon S A,
bottom right British Museum; 42 *bottom right*
Michael Holford, *bottom left*, 45 Ronald Sheridan; 46
Martin von Wagner Museum, Würzburg; 52 Ronald
Sheridan; 53 British Museum; 59 Martin von Wagner
Museum, Würzburg; 60 Michael Holford; 62 Hirmer
Fotoarchiv; 63 *top left* Michael Holford, *bottom right*
British Museum; 69 Sonia Halliday; 70, 71 *bottom*
Ronald Sheridan, *top right* Michael Holford; 73
ZEFA; 75 Ronald Sheridan; 76 Martin von Wagner
Museum, Würzburg; 79 British Museum; 81 Ekdotike
Athenon S A; 82, 83 Ronald Sheridan; 84, 87 Sonia
Halliday; 89 *top left* Michael Holford, *bottom right*
Colorsport.

The publishers also wish to thank the following artists
for contributing to the book:

Jane Cope pp. 28–9, 34–5;
Kevin Maddison pp. 10–11, 24, 25, 26, 30, 38, 45, 46,
47 *bottom*, 50, 56, 58, 59, 68, 70, 72, 74–5, 78, 85;
Malcolm Porter pp. 11, 12, 40, 44, 49, 78, 79, 80, 83;
David Salariya cover and pp. 21 *bottom*, 27, 36–7, 43,
54–5, 61, 66–7, 77;
Richard Scollins pp. 48, 64, 65;
Shirley Willis pp. 20, 21 *top*, 47 *top*, 57.

Kingfisher History Library

THE GREEK WORLD

Anton Powell

Kingfisher Books

CONTENTS

The Greek World

The ancient Greeks were some of the most creative people the world has ever known. Two-and-a-half thousand years ago they had a revolution in thinking. It was as important, perhaps, as the industrial revolution of modern times.

We still use countless words and ideas which the Greeks first thought of. In many countries people proudly call their political system by a Greek name—*democracy*. When we think about *history* or *philosophy* we are doing something invented and named by the Greeks. For entertainment we watch *drama*, often at the *theatre* (two more Greek words). We have even recreated the Olympic games, first staged by the Greeks at Olympia. And indeed the games today are very like the ancient Olympics—exciting and highly political.

The ancient Greek world was lively and inventive for about 2000 years, starting about 1600 BC. Over that period there were many different styles of Greek civilization. There were the Mycenaeans (*circa* 1600–1150 BC), with their great palaces and lovely art. Then came a long Dark Age during which memories of the Mycenaean past were woven into long poems. Some of the poetry, the *Iliad* and *Odyssey*, can still be enjoyed today. At the end of the Dark Age, perhaps in the 700s BC, the Greeks learned to use an alphabet; it is the ancestor of our own.

The age of the greatest creativity was from about 600–300 BC. Athens is the city most famous for developing *demokratia* and drama, history and philosophy. But in many ways the lead had come from eastern Greeks across the Aegean Sea. Sadly, their greatest city—Miletos—was destroyed in the 490s BC by invaders from the neighbouring Persian empire, so we will never know what they might have achieved.

Around 330 BC, the Persians themselves were at last conquered—by a warrior called Alexander, from Macedonia at the edge of the Greek world. He started the spread of Greek language and customs across Asian lands, into much of Russia and India, and almost as far as China. And so, protected by the Libyan desert in the west and by Indian war elephants in the east, the age of Greek science began.

Tiryns
This arched corridor, built of great boulders, is part of the Bronze Age fort of Tiryns, near Mycenae.

Epidauros
The theatre at Epidauros was constructed in the 300s BC. It is superbly built. Drop a coin on the stage and it is heard clearly from the back row.

Poseidonia (Paestum)
This temple in southern Italy reflects the wealth of Greek colonists in the west.

THE GREEK WORLD

5TH CENTURY GREECE

Petra, Jordan
Jordan was part of the huge territory won by Alexander the Great in the late 300s BC. Many buildings at Petra were hewn out of rock. This one is in the Greek style.

Stadium at Delphi
Athletic contests, including the original Olympic games, were held in stadia like this.

Stoa at Athens
A stoa was a long corridor with columns. Men strolled up and down it chatting.

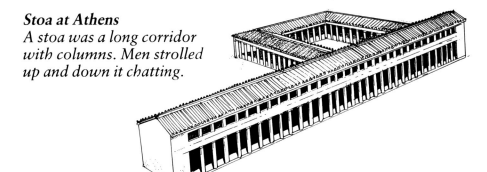

11

The Country

If you fly across the interior of Greece at night, and look down from the plane, you will see hardly any lights below. Very few people live there. It was similar in ancient times. This is because most of inland Greece consists of bare mountain. Little would grow in the interior. Greece, a country so rich in ideas, was very poor in natural resources.

Most Greeks lived near the sea, as they still do. Along the coast there was very often a narrow plain which could be cultivated. Commonly the plain was hemmed in by mountains, and covered only a few square kilometres. The land route to the next coastal town often lay over a mountain. So the Greeks became a people of the sea. Sailing was needed for contact with neighbours, for fishing and for trading at a distance.

The Greeks triumphed over disadvantages of their landscape. For instance, there were few large trees, so timber was in short supply. Greeks reacted by making fine temples and statues of stone. On the shallow soil of hillsides they learned to produce grapes. Their wine-pots, prettily painted, came to be treasured in many lands. And, forced to use the sea, Greeks became the greatest sailors of their day, with bases from Spain to Russia.

Above: A typical scene from the interior of Greece. The ground is dry and rocky, the soil poor. Few people lived in these mountainous areas.

Below: The map shows how flatter, fertile land often lies near the coast. Mainlanders as well as islanders had to communicate by sea.

Timeline

All the events described in this book, and listed here, took place before the birth of Christ. BC stands for "before Christ". Until the 400s BC, all dates are approximate.

BC

Mycenaean Age

1500s	The mainland of southern and central Greece is probably divided into small, rich kingdoms, with palaces at Mycenae, Pylos and elsewhere.
1200s	The kingdoms are threatened. Great defensive walls, and the Lion Gate of Mycenae, are built.
1200	Pylos is attacked and burned.
1150	Mycenae is similarly wrecked. End of the main Mycenaean civilization.

Dark Age and Archaic period

1000	Greeks move eastwards and form colonies on the western coasts of Asia Minor.
early 700s	Olympic Games begin. First writing in the Greek alphabet.
700s	Hesiod composes his poems.
late 700s onwards	There is a widespread Greek movement to colonize the coasts of Sicily, southern Italy and Gaul.
700	Greeks begin to fight in the phalanx formation.
	Tyrants replace the aristocracies in many towns (600s and 500s BC).
600	Greeks first made coins.
500	Great age of the eastern Greeks. Pioneers work in geography, history, philosophy, physics and astronomy.
mid 500s	Start of Sparta's domination of southern Greece.
508–7	Beginnings of Athenian *demokratia*.
490s	Eastern Greeks, led by Miletos, revolt in vain against the spreading Persian empire.

Classical period

490	Persians raid Athens, but are defeated at Marathon.
480–79	The great Persian invasion of Greece. Battles of Salamis and Plataia.
477	A new alliance, led by Athens, is formed to raid the Persian empire.
450s–440s	The alliance turns into an Athenian empire.
447 onwards	Construction of the Parthenon at Athens.
mid and late 400s	The great age of Athenian drama. Aiskhylos, Sophokles and Euripides write tragedy. Aristophanes writes comedy.
431	Sparta attacks Athens and begins the Peloponnesian war. Thucydides the Athenian begins work on his history of the conflict.
415	Athens tries to conquer Sicily.
413	Athens' entire invasion force is destroyed by Syracuse.
404	Athens is starved into surrender.
404–371	The Spartan empire. Sparta's tiny population has difficulty running it.
399	Sokrates swallows poison in Athens.
early 300s	Plato teaches philosophy in Athens.
371	Thebans overwhelm Spartans at the Battle of Leuktra.
370 or 369	Thebes frees the Messenian helots, breaking Sparta's power for ever.
338	Thebes and Athens are defeated by Philip of Macedon at the battle of Khaironeia. Philip dominates Greece.
336	Murder of Philip. His son, Alexander, succeeds him.
334–1	Alexander invades and conquers the Persian empire.
323	Alexander dies at Babylon. His generals divide up his empire. Seleukos gets Asia, Ptolemy Egypt.

Hellenistic period

200s	The great age of Greek science, centred on Alexandria in Egypt.
100s	Rome gains power in Asia.
30	The last ruler of Ptolemy's family, Cleopatra VII, loses her kingdom to Rome.

The Evidence

How do we know about the Greeks? Where does our information come from? For the earliest times, the period of Mycenaean civilization and the Dark Age which followed, most of our knowledge comes from poetry and archaeology. For later times, including the Classical period, there are also works of prose written by Greeks. The poetry and the prose were copied by hand through the Roman period, into the late Middle Ages and until printing was invented.

Clues from poetry

How is poetry important? Think of the English rhyme:

"Hickory, dickory, dock,
The mouse ran up the clock."

The first line is nonsense but it has been passed on accurately for generations. This has happened partly because of the rhyming syllables "dock" and "clock", and partly because of the rhythm:

da-didi da-didi da
di-da di-da di-da.

If the nonsense syllables had not been in poetry, no one would have remembered them for five minutes!

Greek poetry hardly ever used rhyme but it did use strict and complicated rhythms. Words which fitted these rhythms could be remembered and passed on accurately for centuries, even without the aid of writing. So the poems preserve precious detail about the past.

The oldest surviving Greek poems are the *Iliad* and the *Odyssey*. They tell of a world of rich palaces and beautiful princesses, of warrior-kings, war chariots and helmets made of boars' tusks. All these things existed during the Mycenaean period, which ended about 1150 BC. When Greeks heard the poems much later during the Classical period (400s and 300s BC), the palaces were in ruins. Only the poems kept colourful details alive.

Buried evidence

In the 1800s, a German businessman named Heinrich Schliemann set out to find the lost world of the poems. The *Iliad* had described a great war at a fortress named Troy, near the north-western tip of Asia Minor. By digging there, Schliemann found the remains of an ancient fortress: almost certainly the original Troy. Still following the information in the *Iliad* and *Odyssey*, he dug on the Greek mainland at Mycenae. There he found great treasures, as we shall see on page 23.

The poems also told of a palace at Pylos. In the 1930s an American archaeologist, Carl Blegen, searched for it. But there were many sites called Pylos; which one was meant in the poems? Blegen judged that the Pylos in Messenia (in south-western Greece) was the likeliest. But there were no ruins to be seen. Trusting his judgement, he dug a trench to explore. It ran straight into the buried remains of a palace.

More important still, Blegen's trench entered a room where palace officials had kept written records. How they wrote, and how their script was deciphered, we shall see on page 26. But the records made it certain that the rulers who lived in the palaces used the Greek language, as the poems had suggested. They gave details which matched information in the poems. Archaeology, guided by

A diver finds an amphora, a storage vessel for wine or oil, lost in ancient times when a ship sank.

The Akropolis of Athens, still fortified by ancient walls and crowned by temples. It is evidence of the wealth of Athens' empire.

clues in the poems, allows us to see for ourselves things which the Greek poems remembered in words.

Archaeological evidence leaves Greece
The archaeological evidence on Greece is now scattered in many countries. There are hundreds of museums throughout Europe and North America where we can see interesting and attractive objects made by the Greeks. How did these objects come to be so scattered?

Some things, like painted pottery, were exported by the ancient Greeks themselves. (There is more about pottery on pages 18 and 19.) Later the Romans ruled Greece. They admired Greek art and shipped many treasures, especially statues, to Italy. Some of these have remained in Italy. (A few of the ships sank. Underwater archaeology is now recovering pottery and statues from the sea bed.)

In the early 1800s, when the Turks ruled Greece, people from Britain and Germany were given permission to remove some of the finest remaining sculpture from Greek temples. It is still in Britain and Germany today. Understandably, the Greeks would now like it back.

Rich and poor
Archaeology tells us more about rich towns than poor ones. Athens, which ran a profitable empire, still has lovely temples to show—like the Parthenon. Sparta, a much poorer city, now has few remains even though it managed to conquer Athens.

Similarly, archaeology reveals more about rich individuals than about poor ones. Rich people's possessions were made from better quality (and therefore longer-lasting) materials. For example, stone palaces last longer than mud cottages. There are a few exceptions, however. Excavations at the abandoned northern city of Olynthos have revealed some mud houses belonging to the poor.

Many decrees, inscribed on stone, survive from Athens. One of them tells of land given to the poor. Badly-spelled messages for the gods, scratched on pieces of lead at a shrine, show how ordinary people worried about making a living.

Evidence from historians

From the 500s BC onwards, several Greeks wrote long works of history in prose. Two of the most important of these books have survived. They are by Herodotos and Thucydides. They tell us so much about the Greek world that, even today, scholars are still able to learn new things by looking closely at what the two writers said.

Herodotos was born soon after 500 BC in Halikarnassos, a Greek town in western Asia Minor. In his early years Halikarnassos was under Persian control. This may have helped Herodotos, because his book was about the wars between Persia and the Greeks. His mixed background made it possible for him to be fair to both sides. He did not view the Persians as a mad and wicked enemy, as many other Greeks did. Herodotos respected the Persians and this made it possible for him to understand them. Most of our knowledge of the Persian wars is drawn from his book.

Herodotos also respected his readers, allowing them to decide for themselves about stories which he doubted. He reports a tale about Phoenician seamen who claimed to have sailed round Africa. They said that when they sailed round southern Africa, the sun was on their right hand (that is, to the north of them). Herodotos did not believe this. But he still recorded it, leaving it for his readers to judge. We can now see that the detail about the sun is important evidence. It suggests that the men did get south of the Equator.

Tablets of clay, bearing the earliest known Greek script—Linear B, from the Bronze Age. Enemy fire baked the clay and preserved it.

Unlike Herodotos, the historian Thucydides had little time for stories. He knew that the more entertaining a story was, the more likely it was to have been made up. Thucydides took pride in the accuracy of his work, boasting that it might last for ever. He did not leave his readers to judge between conflicting accounts, as Herodotos had sometimes done. Thucydides made up *his* mind and gave only the version he believed in.

Thucydides' theme was the great war between Athens and Sparta, the Peloponnesian war of 431–404 BC. He himself fought for a time in it as an Athenian general. His book also gives precious information about social life and religion.

Archaeology provides evidence that Thucydides' writing was accurate. For example, he

This sculpted stone of a cat and dog fighting was built into a wall, as Thucydides described.

Miltiades probably wore this helmet while commanding at the battle of Marathon. It was found at Olympia, where it had been presented to the god Zeus. Miltiades' name is still legible.

women's skin and the boldness of animals in the streets of Athens. Tragic drama sometimes reflects Athenian daily life. Female characters on stage occasionally complain of their lack of freedom.

Much colourful information about Athens comes from the comic plays of Aristophanes. He tells us of Athenians waking before dawn, bitten by bed-bugs in their crowded little houses. He describes noisy quarrels in the streets. When the men of Athens were slow to enter their assembly, to decide what the city should do, Aristophanes tells how they were forced to hurry. A rope, dipped in red paint, herded them towards the assembly. Anyone who did not hurry got paint on his clothes and had to pay a fine.

Heinrich Schliemann excavated at Troy and Mycenae. This photograph shows his Greek wife, Sophie, wearing ancient jewellery which he found while excavating.

records that the Athenians used even sculpted stones in their hurry to rebuild the city wall after the Persian invasion. Archaeologists have found such sculpted stones where he said they were. Astronomy, too, supports Thucydides. He often mentions eclipses, because many Greeks believed them to be signs from the gods. Astronomers today are able to confirm that these eclipses took place when Thucydides said they did.

Perhaps one of the most important things which Thucydides shows us is that the minds of the Greeks worked similarly to our own. For example, Thucydides says that they were often misled by wishful thinking when undertaking some dangerous action. They were like people today who say that bad things "won't happen to *me*". Thucydides records that when Athens was struck by plague, many people thought it was sent by a god. This still happens today sometimes, when a disaster occurs or a horrible disease hits a community.

The Greeks were not like us in *every* way. But Thucydides shows they were similar enough for us usually to understand them.

Other sources

Speeches which survive from Athenian lawcourts give us details of family life, trade and crime. Books by Plato and Aristotle deal with politics and philosophy, and also give lively details (as we shall see) about such matters as the paleness of

Pictures on Pots

One of the most interesting ways to find out about the Greeks is to look at the pictures they made on their pottery. Many of these paintings are still clear and colourful after more than 2500 years.

The painted scenes are often connected with the way the pots were used. Pottery made to hold wine often has scenes of men drinking at parties (see page 36). Large water-pitchers have scenes of women going to a spring (see the picture on page 46, which is based on a Greek painting). The pictures can often show more clearly than words how Greeks lived, worked and played.

Some of these painted pots are still being discovered—often by tomb robbers. These people prod the ground with long rods. When the rod slips easily through the earth it is a sign that there may be a burial chamber below. The robbers dig, hoping to find pottery and other treasures buried with some rich person in ancient times. They sell their finds to private collectors and museums.

Archaeologists can usually tell roughly when a pot was made, and the pictures tell us what was considered important at that time. From the last years of Mycenaean Greece, when enemy forces were approaching, there is a vase showing foot-soldiers marching off to defend their town. Later, during the Dark Age, crudely painted figures are shown attending the funerals of aristocrats. We can tell from the number of horses shown on these pots how much these animals were valued.

Then comes fine pottery from Corinth (especially in the 600s BC). It shows bright and sophisticated designs of oriental monsters, including the Egyptian sphinx. So we can guess who the Corinthians were trading with. One Corinthian pot shows armoured foot-soldiers advancing in lines. This tells us that this style of fighting was being used by the mid-600s BC. The loveliest vases of all came from Athens and were made in huge numbers from 600 to 400 BC. They are painted with varied scenes from mythology, everyday life and war.

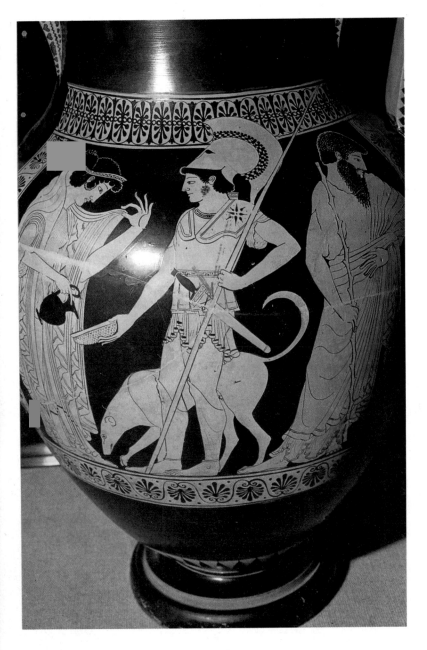

A hoplite leaves home for war. The vase-painter has shown a family scene which must have been common during the Archaic and Classical periods. (The dog is the painter's way of telling people that the scene takes place at home.) The warrior's wife pours wine into a ritual dish, from which it falls onto the ground as a sacrifice. They are praying to one of the gods that the warrior will return safely. The other man is probably the warrior's father. Painting on a beard was a Greek artist's way of showing that a man was elderly or middle-aged. This man's age explains why he himself is not going to war.

In this scene from myth, Atalante, a female athlete, wrestles with a male, Peleus. As often on Athenian pre-Classical vases, the female has white flesh and the male has black. This reflects the fact that in real life Greek men saw more of the sun.

This painting from a pot shows a potter at work, shaping his clay on a wheel. The potter was usually a different person from the vase painter, and seems to have made more profit from his work. Fine pottery was exported as far as Italy and Gaul, often carrying inscriptions about the more famous members of Athenian society.

A wounded warrior is bandaged by a companion. Pain from the wound may explain why the man looks away. Each soldier wears the breastplate of a hoplite. The metal helmet of the man on the right has horsehair plumes, to make him look taller in battle. Below the waist each man is almost naked. Some of the nastier wounds were received here.

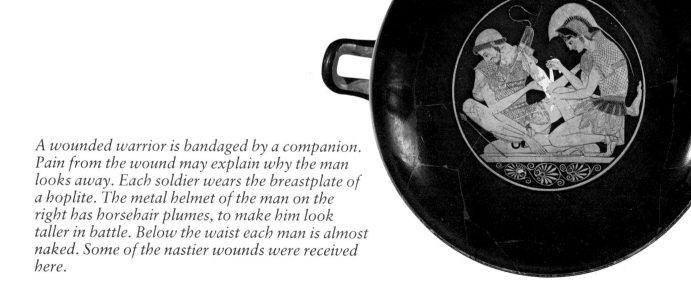

The Mycenaean World

For us, prehistoric Greece bursts into colour and life around 1600 BC. Then began the civilization known today as Mycenaean. Mycenae itself may not have been the capital of an empire. Many rich little towns, perhaps independent, shared a style of art and building—and the Greek language. But so striking are the remains of Mycenae that its name has been given to the whole civilization.

Mycenaean settlements often began as villages on a hillside. Only in the last period of the civilization were great fortresses built, as at Mycenae, Tiryns and Gla. In many ways the style of art and of palace buildings was borrowed from the older Minoan culture of Crete. (The Minoans may

The citadel of Mycenae today, viewed from the west. The defensive wall, grave circle and remains of palace buildings can be seen quite clearly.

THE MYCENAEAN WORLD

not have spoken Greek though their great city of Knossos was for a time under Greek control.) Mycenaean towns were ruled by a wealthy few— probably by royal families. These rulers spent much of their people's wealth on the products of craftsmen, some of the finest builders, artists and metalworkers of the ancient world. There was trade with remote lands; modern tests have shown that amber was brought from northern Europe, near the Baltic Sea. Ivory for carving came from Africa. The Mycenaeans kept written records, on clay and probably also on papyrus. This was similar to paper, made from a reed and imported from Egypt.

Right: Map of the "Mycenaean world" during the late Bronze Age (1600–1150 BC). A reconstruction of the fortress at Mycenae in the 1200s BC.

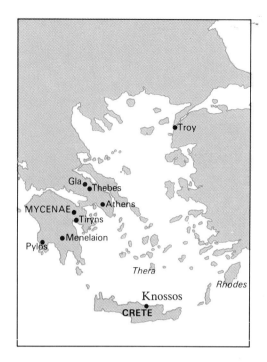

THE MYCENAEAN WORLD

A palace for a dead ruler of Mycenae—a beehive tomb. Inside was a vast domed chamber with a small side-room for the body.

Beehive tombs

Before the age of the fortresses, Mycenaean builders showed their skill in the construction of "beehive tombs". These were made of stone blocks, shaped to curve smoothly into a great dome. The interior of one of them—the Treasury of Atreus—is over 13 metres in height and 14 metres in diameter. (You can see it in the picture above.) Not until Roman times, over 1500 years later, did builders elsewhere in Europe manage to create such a large unsupported chamber.

Some of the royal dead who were placed in Mycenaean graves were provided with food. One corpse was left a box of oysters to enjoy! This may give us a clue as to why beehive tombs were constructed. Since it was believed—or hoped—that there was a life after death, dead royalty would need stylish surroundings. The beehive tombs may have been built to be the palaces of the underworld. Through remaining under the earth, these tombs have been better preserved than the rooms built above ground. They give us some idea of how much wealth and craftsmanship must have been lavished on the palaces of the living.

The beehive tombs also suggest that Mycenaean society was tightly organized for the benefit of its rulers. Unlike farming, garment-making or house-building, the construction of elaborate graves did not create things to meet the bodily needs of daily life. Yet, at times, much of the wealth and the skilled labour of the society was spent on rulers' burial places. In other respects, Mycenaean life must have been productive and well organized. Otherwise the remaining labour and wealth would not have been sufficient to support the society. Written records show that the production and distribution of goods were carefully controlled by officials in the palaces.

Fortresses built by giants?

When Greeks of later times looked at the ruined walls of Mycenaean fortresses, they could not believe that ordinary people had built them. They called the walls "cyclopean" because, surely, giants like the Cyclops must have lifted the boulders into place. In reality, great gangs of Mycenaean workmen did the job, perhaps using levers and wooden platforms to raise the stones. Outer surfaces of the walls were made smooth by painstaking work. Tools made of iron were not yet widely used. (Mycenaean civilization forms part of what archaeologists call the Bronze Age.) The stones may have been smoothed by saws of bronze, used with wet sand to help the saws bite.

Mycenae Rich in Gold

In many aristocracies down the ages, women of the ruling families have held powerful and interesting positions. One Mycenaean wall-painting shows women riding in a chariot. Another seems to portray a woman hunting a boar with a spear. Women are also shown taking part in ceremonies. They wear intricate and expensive clothes in bright colours such as red and blue.

Stories were told later about a King Agamemnon of Mycenae, who had led an army drawn from many parts of Greece. His career was much influenced by women, as we shall see on pages 28 and 29. In the 19th century the romance of these tales led Heinrich Schliemann to excavate at Mycenae—with glittering results.

In the poetry of Homer, Mycenae is described as "rich in gold". When Schliemann found the golden mask shown below, he sent a telegram saying excitedly (but probably wrongly), "I have gazed on the face of Agamemnon."

Mycenaean craftsmen worked gold with great delicacy and success. They made flowers of gold, probably as ornaments for women. Golden cups and pourers were moulded to represent animals. Royalty might use them at banquets or for pouring sacrifices of wine to the gods. (The gods were modelled closely on humans, and so they got thirsty at times!) There were also golden signet rings, such as the one shown below. When the ring was pressed against a seal of clay or wax, it left its picture there. If someone broke the seal, perhaps to enter a storeroom or to open a secret chest, their entry would be noticed—they could not make a copy of the seal to replace the one they had broken.

So many peoples have valued gold, as the Mycenaeans did, that we may forget to ask why. Part of the answer is that gold does not easily lose its bright colour—unlike other metals. Even when it is taken from an ancient hiding-place, gold still glitters. Also important is the fact that gold is usually very scarce. Poor people, even at Mycenae, could not afford it. So, to own a lot of gold, then as now, was a way of showing that you were a richer and grander person than most.

Left: This is the finest of several death masks from Mycenae. A death mask may have recorded the looks of a king and given an elegant new face at a time when death had made the real face unpleasant.
Below: A Mycenaean signet ring of gold. Women in tight-waisted clothes seem to be performing some sort of religious rite.

The Warrior Kings

The king of a Mycenaean city needed to impress. He had to intimidate the rulers of other cities—and perhaps his own subjects. So he needed a reputation as a brave and warlike man. It also helped if he was tall. Then he would make a fine, easily-seen figure on a battlefield, and would look superior when he walked among his subjects in peacetime.

The skeletons of rulers and their relatives, found in graves at Mycenae, suggest that they were indeed taller on average than their subjects. This has been true of aristocrats in many societies. They are well fed in childhood. And, as adults, the males have their pick of tall women to marry. This helps towards the production of tall offspring.

The skeletons of the Mycenaean nobles also show that they suffered many broken bones. The aristocrats seem to have led violently active lives. Bones might break in accidents with horses and chariots, and especially during a hunt. Much art of the palaces shows scenes from hunting. To kill a lion, using a spear and a figure-of-eight shield, was both thrilling and useful for a nobleman. It had much of the excitement of war but was a little less dangerous. It trained the body in warlike skills. And, perhaps most importantly, it made people think that aristocrats were hard, courageous men. Discontented subjects might think twice about attacking a ruler who could kill lions!

Lion-killing also helped to justify the ruler's power. Farm animals were threatened by the lion. If the king or his relatives killed this dangerous beast, their subjects would see that they contributed something useful to the wealth of the community.

So the lion became one of the favourite figures in Mycenaean art. One royal dagger blade showed a hunted lion in gold (see below). A container for

Above: An ivory model, made in Mycenaean times, of a warrior's head protected by a boars'-tusk helmet.

liquid was made of gold in the shape of a lion's head. And the fortified palace at Mycenae had two large stone lions to guard the entrance (see facing page).

Another dangerous animal, glorious to hunt, was the wild boar. Its slashing tusks could inflict fatal wounds. (Later poetry, set in the Mycenaean era, described the hero Odysseus as permanently scarred by a boar's tusk.) The tusks of a dead boar were sliced lengthways, and the slices were attached to a cap of cloth to form a warrior's helmet. To get enough tusks to make one helmet, a man might need to kill several boars. So the helmet had two uses. It gave protection and it also suggested that its wearer was a distinguished spearsman.

THE MYCENAEAN WORLD

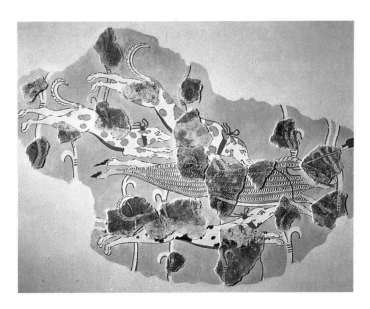

The Lion Gate

The Lion Gate was the great entrance to the citadel of Mycenae. Today the lions have lost their heads but otherwise they stand above the huge stone lintel as they have for over 3000 years.

The gateway, and the boulders forming the walls which led to it, were meant to give an impression of strength. It was hoped that enemies would look on them and despair. But when people boast of their strength it is often because they are nervous. And these fortifications were built at a time when the Mycenaeans felt weaker than before. For about 300 years Mycenae may have been secure enough not to need a large defensive wall around it. But around 1300 BC the ruler became so afraid of attack that he spent the labour of his people on the massive project of wall-building.

Behind the lions was a hollow, to reduce the weight on the lintel and prevent it cracking. Beneath the lintel were gates, probably of wood and bronze. The gate has gone but in the stonework there is still the socket for the great timber which once barred the gate. The approach to the gates was flanked on both sides by a wall. In this way, enemies assaulting the gate would find it difficult to protect themselves with their shields. They would be caught in the crossfire, with spears, arrows and stones coming at them from two or three sides at once.

Above left: Part of a Mycenaean wall-painting showing a boar hunt.
Below: A chariot enters Mycenae by the Lion Gate. Sentries, by the gate and on the wall, remind us of the enemy who soon overwhelmed these new fortifications.

Keeping Records

Deciphering the Mycenaean script

Many tablets of baked clay engraved with writing have been found at Mycenae, Pylos and Knossos. On some there were drawings of men or women, horses or chariots, but there were also signs in a mysterious script which scholars named Linear B (see above). Around 1950 an English architect, Michael Ventris, deciphered them in his spare time. There were about 89 different signs—too many for the script to be an alphabet. Ventris realized that each sign represented a syllable. Using code-breaking techniques, he grouped signs which probably shared a particular consonant,

A scribe writes on a clay tablet. He is recording the contents of a Mycenaean palace storeroom.

and others which probably shared a particular vowel. Then he experimented with the idea that the language was Greek. Quickly a host of Greek words was deciphered, and some matched the drawings perfectly. The mystery was solved.

What the tablets tell us

The Linear B tablets are palace records. They show what was in the storeroom, such as weapons and chariot wheels. They refer to the ruler of the palace as the *wanax* or "king" and they record the goods which people brought him as tax. Gods and goddesses are named, some of whom the Greeks went on worshipping for almost another 2000 years—Zeus and Hera, Athena, Artemis and Poseidon. Ordinary people are mentioned, and even the cattle are named—Dapple and Darkie, Whitefoot and Blondie.

End of the Mycenaean World

The fall of a Mycenaean palace. In the distance, buildings burn as captured women are led off by the conquerors.

The fires which baked the Linear B tablets were probably those in which the great palaces themselves were destroyed. These fires were not accidental. In many parts of Greece, Mycenaean settlements were wrecked during the same period, perhaps about 1200 BC. Arrowheads and human bones have been found outside the palace at Pylos, suggesting a battle there. It is not clear who the enemy was. Was it local people? In later times poor Greek citizens often took arms against the local rich people. However, one great Mycenaean structure, a wall about six kilometres long blocking the Isthmos of Corinth, suggests that invaders from the north were feared.

Around 1200 BC there were invasions and violent upheavals in much of the eastern Mediterranean world. The great Hittite empire of Asia Minor fell at that time. The fortress of Troy was captured (by the Mycenaeans, later Greeks thought). And Egypt was invaded by "sea peoples". We know that the ruler of Pylos expected trouble to arrive from the sea, for Linear B tablets from Pylos record the sending out of rowers and of watchers to guard the coasts. Fear of catastrophe may help to explain the many sacrifices that are mentioned on the tablets. The Greeks, like people today, prayed most when they were frightened.

The Greek Tradition

Iliad and *Odyssey*

After the fall of the Mycenaean towns, the Greek world passed into a period of which we know little—a Dark Age. Population and wealth declined. There was no great building or rich craftsmanship. The art of writing was lost. Greeks speaking a dialect known as Dorian came to dominate the Peloponnese. Other Greeks, using the Ionian dialect, moved east to settle on the western coast of Asia Minor and its nearby islands.

People in the Dark Age did not forget everything about the Mycenaean past. Long "epic" poems told of Mycenae and its treasure, and of the Mycenaean palace at Pylos. Colourful details were remembered. The poems mention the boars' tusk helmets, "tower-tall" shields and ornamental metalwork. They even recall the arrangements for having a bath in a Mycenaean palace.

Epic poetry was composed in strict metre. Poets were illiterate, making up verse in their heads. To compose long and original stories on the spot, fitting everything into the metre, would have been too much of a strain. Instead, a poet combined verses of his own with verses learned from other poets. Some of these inherited lines passed down the centuries. Embedded in them were details about the Mycenaeans.

The *Iliad* and the *Odyssey* are epics from the Dark Age. Later Greeks believed they were composed by a man named Homer, though we have seen that many people down the years helped to form them. They are poems about warrior aristocrats who attacked Troy (also called "Ilion"). The *Iliad* tells how the best fighter, Achilles, lost his beloved woman, Briseis, to King Agamemnon. Achilles went on strike, refusing to fight. The Trojans, led by Hector, were then able to do terrible things to Agamemnon's forces, until Achilles once more came out to fight.

The *Odyssey* is about the return of Odysseus to his island home, after the ten-year siege of Troy. It is an adventure story. Some of Odysseus' men are eaten by the Cyclops; others are turned into animals by the witch Circe. But, after a shipwreck, he regains his home and his wife Penelope.

1. *Three goddesses—Hera, Athena and Aphrodite—competed in beauty. Paris of Troy, a mortal, judged them. He chose Aphrodite as the winner and she promised to give him Helen, the superbly beautiful wife of King Menelaos, as a reward.*

2. *Helen ran off with Paris to Troy. Menelaos's brother, King Agamemnon, led a great force against the city to get her back. Here Achilles, Agamemnon's best warrior, kills Hector who was the champion of Troy.*

28

3. The long siege of Troy was ended by a trick. The attackers pretended to depart and left behind a huge wooden horse. The curious Trojans took it inside the city walls—but hidden inside were some of Agamemnon's soldiers.

5. Agamemnon was not so lucky. Before he left for the war, he had killed his daughter as a sacrifice to help the campaign against Troy. In revenge, his wife Clytaemnestra and her lover murdered him on his return to Mycenae.

4. At last Menelaos had his unfaithful wife back in his power. He came to kill her. But, Greek poets said, "he saw her beauty and threw his sword away". Helen became his queen again.

6. On his journey home, Odysseus listened to the Sirens—monsters whose sweet singing lured sailors to their deaths. Here his men have plugged their ears and tied Odysseus up for safety.

Stories of War, Farming and Fishing

In the *Iliad* the main characters are aristocrats. The ordinary soldiers of the Trojan War are described only briefly—at one point they are likened to flies swarming round a milk pail. Most of the poem's hearers, however, were probably ordinary people such as farmers and shepherds, fishermen and woodcutters. Scholars have found a way of using the *Iliad* to reveal how these ordinary people lived during the Dark Age.

The main story of the *Iliad* is one of war. Death in battle is described in great detail, perhaps even gleefully. For example:

> "He fell on his back in the dust, stretching out his hands towards his comrades, gasping. The man who had hit him, Peiros, ran up and struck him with a spear near his navel. Out poured all his guts onto the ground, and darkness came over his eyes."

For the Dark Age audience, however, these were details of war from a bygone age. To make it easier for them to follow, the poem compares the fighting with scenes familiar to the hearers—scenes from their own lives. These comparisons, known as similes, are often long and full of detail. Through them we can build up a picture of Dark Age life, poor but peaceful, in the countryside.

Where they lived

Two similes in the *Iliad* may give us a clue as to where the original Greek audience lived. Winds

Safe around the fire in winter, they enjoy hearing of shipwrecks and the capture of cities, of beautiful princesses who caused destruction, and of wounded men lying in agony on the battlefield.

A Mycenaean cup made of gold. It shows men struggling to control a bull.

coming from north of the Aegean Sea and heading south-eastwards are said to blow seaweed to the shore. The shore of Asia Minor fits this description best. Also, the audience is expected to be familiar with the noisy flocks of birds by the River Kaystrios, which is in western Asian Minor.

Glimpses of ordinary life

Other similes in the poem describe incidents from everyday life. One compares a handsome young warrior, falling with a spear in his neck, to a young tree destroyed by the wind.

"Like a flourishing young olive plant which a man nourishes in a lonely pasture, where water in plenty bubbles up... It sways in every wind and teems with white blossom. But a sudden dark storm comes; the wind blows it from its trench and leaves it flat upon the ground."

We can guess that there were gardeners in the audience, familiar with this sad experience.

At another point in the poem the shield of Achilles is said to flash into the distance,

"like the firelight from a lonely sheepfold high in the mountains, seen by sailors who are being driven unwillingly out to sea by the winds, away from their friends."

There were evidently sailors in the audience who knew the painful beauty of that distant sight, and understood the yearning for firelight and security.

The fall of another young soldier is compared with that of a poplar tree which a chariot-maker

fells with his gleaming axe. A dance in a circle is likened to the smooth turning of a potter's wheel. A battle, poised between two enemies of equal power, is said to be similar to the precisely balanced scales of a woman dealing in wool (who works for shamefully little to support her children). So here we have information about three different kinds of craftworker from the Dark Age.

Other similes refer to children. The god Apollo is said to knock down a wall as easily as a child at the seaside kicks down a sandcastle. Warriors streaming out to fight are likened to wasps whose nest has been attacked by boys. And there is a picture of a little girl, running along at her mother's side and asking to be picked up.

"She catches at her mother's robe, trying to hold her back as she hurries along, and looks up at her in tears, to be picked up."

The poet repeats himself, to copy the girl: "Pick me up, Mummy, pick me up".

The world of the Homeric similes is remote in time—but it is a world we can still recognize.

A vase painting showing a Greek fisherman using rod and line. The artist has included an octopus— still a favourite Greek food today.

Homeric Gods and Goddesses

Homer's divinities

The *Iliad* and *Odyssey* tell of gods and goddesses who are like a large, quarrelsome family. Zeus is at its head but his wife, Hera, sometimes opposes him. Two of his children, the elegant Apollo and the warrior goddess Athena, fight on opposite sides in the Trojan War. Aphrodite fights too, but she is the goddess of love and of little use on the battlefield. She is even wounded by a mortal, Diomedes. She doesn't bleed, however, as immortals do not have blood. Instead out comes a mysterious substance called *ichor*.

Aphrodite deceives her husband, the blacksmith god Hephaistos, and has a love affair with Ares, the god of war. The lovers are caught together and the gods come to laugh at them. The goddesses, however, are more discreet and do not look. When Hera deceives Zeus she dresses up to make herself more attractive to him. He tells her she is even more beautiful than his other lovers, then tactlessly reminds her of who they all were.

In other words, these divinities resemble human rulers; they are selfish and capable of making mistakes. Their chief is a male and the females are expected to be modest because that was how things were in Greek society. When we see how the immortals entertained themselves with feasting and violence, intrigue and love affairs, we can guess that this was how mortal rulers had their fun.

But in some ways the divinities were superior to human aristocrats. They had qualities which aristocrats would have liked. Mycenaean rulers hoped to live after death in their palatial tombs with their grave goods. So gods and goddesses were immortal. During the Bronze Age, Mycenaean lords lived in palaces on low hills. So Homer's divinities have a palace in which even the floor is made of bronze, on top of soaring Mount Olympos. Homer's descriptions of these immortals help us to reconstruct both the lives and the fantasies of wealthy people in early Greece.

Ideas change

The rich, living in relative security, wanted adventure and entertainment, and so their gods did too. But the poor had other ideas. Their lives already contained more than enough risk, especially of hunger and ill treatment. They dreamed of less selfish divinities who would give protection to ordinary people.

In the 700s BC, at the same time as Homeric poetry was taking its final shape, there lived another important poet. His name was Hesiod. He resented the aristocratic way of life and wrote about Zeus as a just, avenging god. This idea of Zeus was to form part of Greek religion for centuries, as we shall see on pages 72–73.

The warrior goddess Athena was Zeus's favourite daughter. He called her "dear owl eyes". (The owl was her symbol.) The legend of her birth is extraordinary and violent. Before birth she was carried not in the body of a female but in that of Zeus. She was born when Hephaistos, the smith god, split Zeus's head with an axe. Out leaped Athena, fully grown, in armour and shouting her war-cry.

During the Trojan War, gods and goddesses took sides. For example, Aphrodite and Apollo fought for the Trojans, Athena and Hera supported the army of Agamemnon. But it was fated that Troy should fall, so even gods were unable to save the city. This vase painting shows scenes from the capture of Troy. One of the conquerors can be seen holding up the infant Astyanax by the leg. He is about to kill him by smashing his head on the ground. (Astyanax was the grandson of King Priam of Troy.) In the scene below, Menelaos (far left) is angrily approaching Helen (centre), his runaway wife for whom the long war has been fought. Helen is shown baring her beautiful pale body, to remind Menelaos of what he would lose by killing her. She is saved by the goddess Aphrodite, who stands between her and Menelaos, raising a shield to block his way. It was Aphrodite's fault, after all, that Helen was given to Paris and Menelaos lost his wife.

Gods and goddesses of Olympos

Zeus: King of the Olympian gods and the dispenser of justice. He was god of the sky and controlled the weather, especially storms and thunderbolts.

Hera: First love and long-suffering wife of Zeus. She cheats him at times to get her own way.

Apollo: Son of Zeus and god of music, poetry and medicine (though he also sent plagues to kill people).

Artemis: Daughter of Zeus and chaste goddess of the hunt and the moon. She was also a goddess of death and had an interest in childbirth.

Athena: Born from the forehead of Zeus, the goddess of wisdom, war and crafts. She took a special interest in the welfare of Athens and its citizens.

Dionysos: Son of Zeus and god of wine and intoxication. People celebrated his festivals with wild parties, and with strange wanderings in the countryside.

Poseidon: Brother of Zeus and god of the sea, earthquakes, and horses.

Aphrodite: Goddess of beauty and love. She was awarded the golden apple by Paris, an event which led to the Trojan War.

Demeter: The goddess of grain. Her mourning for her lost daughter caused winter; her daughter's reappearance from the Underworld brought spring.

Hermes: The messenger of the gods. He was god of herdsmen, travellers, and liars. He took people's souls to the Underworld.

Hades: The ruler of the gloomy Underworld, also called Hades, where the spirits of the dead lived.

The Archaic Age

Aristocrats and Horses

At the end of the Dark Age it was normal for a Greek town to be ruled by a few wealthy families. In many cases a family probably owed its power to one energetic ancestor, a man who had grown prosperous through war or trade and had passed on his fortune to his descendants. They came to own much of the land in their state and lived stylishly on the wealth which their tenants and slaves produced. To make sure that their families remained powerful, they often arranged for their children to marry into families of similar standing. Marriage between members of two powerful families might be rather like the making of an alliance between two little states. The bride and groom married for power, status and wealth rather than for love.

These ruling families came to be called the "best people"—*aristoi* in Greek—from which we get the word "aristocrat". They were also called the "people with famous names". They were very proud of themselves, and a possession in which they took especial pride was the horse.

To keep fine horses was known to be expensive. So, like powerful cars today, horses were a way of displaying wealth. Also, before the coming of hoplite (foot-soldier) fighting, horses dominated the battlefield (see page 42). The man who rode

An Athenian vase showing a charioteer. Chariots were used for show and for racing even after they ceased to be used in battle.

his own warhorse could move much faster than a foot-soldier and was more frightening to an enemy. And, if his side was defeated, he could escape quickly. Greek vase painters and sculptors often portrayed the horse as a symbol of wealth and power.

THE ARCHAIC AGE

Horsey names

As an additional badge of status, many Greeks were given a horsey name. The word for horse was *hippo-*. (The word "hippopotamus" originally meant a river-horse.) *Hippo-* is one of the commonest elements in the Greek names we know of. *Hippokrates*, for example, meant "horse-strength" and *Philippos* (Philip) meant "horse-lover".

In the age of Athenian democracy, a comic poet described a mother who still had aristocratic tastes. She wanted to give her baby son a *hippo-* name. And she looked forward to the day when he could drive a horse-drawn chariot like his uncle Megakles ("Big-Name"). But the child's father had more democratic ideals. He wanted his son to grow up thrifty. So the parents compromised and called their son *Pheidippides*, "Spare-the-Horses".

Entertainment

The historian Herodotos gives a pleasant picture of the way aristocrats might live. Kleisthenes, ruler of the state of Sikyon, wanted an eminent man as husband for his daughter. So he issued a general invitation, and many distinguished and wealthy men came to his court from various cities of Greece. Among them were Athenians named Megakles and Hippokleides, and—from the luxurious western city of Sybaris—Smindyrides, son of Hippokrates.

They were all entertained for a year while they competed at running, wrestling and elegant conversation to show how well brought up they were. Hippokleides was likely to win but at the last moment let himself down. At the final banquet he performed excellently at music and speech-making but then got very drunk. He stood on his head on the table-top and waved his legs in the air.

Aristocrats were often so powerful and confident that they cared little what other people thought. When Hippokleides was told that his behaviour had cost him the marriage, he replied, "That makes no difference to Hippokleides."

Heavy drinking was a well known characteristic of Greek aristocrats. (Poorer people might not have time for a long drinking session. Nor could they afford to lose a day's work because of a hangover.) Kleisthenes was a *tyrannos* (tyrant) and may well have disapproved of certain aristocratic actions, as other *tyrannoi* did. One such ruler placed a double punishment on crimes committed through drunkenness, probably to control aristocratic misbehaviour. So getting drunk in Kleisthenes' presence may have been one of the most tactless things Hippokleides could have done.

The wedding procession of a wealthy couple, copied from a Greek vase. Looking from left to right, the bride's mother or sister sees her off from the door of her home. A woman carries a vessel of sacred water for the marriage. Another woman carries a box containing the bride's dowry, perhaps a large sum of money. The best man carries a blazing torch. The groom steps into the wedding chariot, beside his bride. The new mother-in-law greets the bride, again with a torch—it is evidently night. On the right a man seems to stand by a sacrificial altar, pointing to the groom's house.

Rich Men at Play

A Symposion

Wealthy Greek men often entertained at a special kind of party. It was known as a *symposion*—a "drinking group". The guests lay on couches and one of them was chosen to control the speed at which they all drank their wine. Without his instruction, some men might have got drunk too quickly, while others stayed too sober. If that had happened, the drunken guests and the sober ones would not have found each other very entertaining!

The wine was often drunk from a *kylix*, a broad shallow cup with handles. Inside the *kylix* a scene might be painted; it became visible to the drinker as he tilted and emptied his cup.

The *kylix* was used for a noisy party game—*kottabos*. The drinker held his cup by one handle, then swung it quickly to make the dregs of wine fly across the room. The dregs were meant to hit a dish on a stand. While they were in the air, the drinker called out the name of someone he would like to have as a lover. If his dregs hit the dish and knocked it off, it was thought that his wish would come true.

Wine was served from a great pot known as a *krater*—a "mixing bowl"—where it had been mixed with water. Of course, the more mixing bowls were emptied, the more drunk the guests became. One poet wrote in a comedy that sensible guests went home after three bowls had been drunk. Four bowls, he said, caused drunken play; five caused shouting; six rioting; seven fighting; eight caused people to be locked up; nine made them sick; ten led to madness and to things being thrown about.

While they were fairly sober, guests would often

THE ARCHAIC AGE

entertain each other by making up poetry. Each man would try to match the verse of the man before. Some played musical instruments, such as the lyre and the double flute (*aulos*).

Dancing and music were also provided by professionals, slaves and ex-slaves. These were often attractive young women, highly trained and expensive to hire. They played and danced, acted and did acrobatics. It is easy for us to see why the wives of citizens were not allowed to attend these parties.

We often hear of people today taking part in a *symposium*. (This is the Roman way of spelling "symposion".) A modern symposium is a serious occasion, at which people in suits talk about subjects of importance. They are certainly not expected to get drunk! How did the Greek word for a drinking party come to get this meaning?

In the early 300s BC, the Athenian philosopher Plato wrote a book called *The Symposion*. It was about a party where some of the guests arrived with headaches, from drinking too much at an earlier party. So, instead of drinking heavily and talking about lovers, the guests decided to stay sober and to have a serious discussion about the nature of love itself. Among the speakers was Plato's hero, the philosopher Sokrates: it was said that no one had *ever* seen him drunk. During the discussion, a noisy guest arrived late. He was expecting a *symposion* of the usual kind. He was so drunk that he had to lean on a flute girl, to stop himself falling over. This was the aristocrat Alkibiades. He was quickly told that *this* party was different. It is from Plato's story of a sober party that our word "symposium" has come.

In real life it was probably unusual for party guests to talk about philosophy. But conversation—and grumbling—about politics were common at parties, as they are today. Because *symposia* were mainly for rich and influential men, the guests may often have talked of seizing power by revolution.

Women in the Shadows

Almost all the written information surviving from ancient Greece is the work of men. We rarely hear things from a woman's point of view. A certain amount is known about the lives of women from wealthy families, and of the very different women—often slaves or ex-slaves—who performed at men's parties. But women of these two groups formed only a small minority of the female population. The history of ordinary Greek women is, for us, one long dark age.

Life in the shadows

Plato, an Athenian living in the 300s BC, suggested that many females should be educated and live on terms of equality with males. But this idea was quite unacceptable to most Greeks. Even women, Plato feared, would reject the thought of sharing the men's world. Women, he explained, were used to a "life in the shadows". What did he mean?

On many Greek vases, men are shown with black flesh and women with white (see page 19). Although this exaggerates the difference in appearance between the sexes, women in real life *were* much paler than men. This was because women's skin got much less of the sun than men's. Women stayed at home much more. And when they did get out they would often hide themselves from men's eyes (and from the sun) with long robes and a headdress—rather as many Muslim women still do today.

To be pale was fashionable for a woman. It suggested she came from a wealthy family. In contrast, a dark skin was a sign that a woman worked in the sun, at the market or in the fields, and only poor women did that.

As make-up, women often used powder of white lead to make their skin paler. This may seem strange today when a suntan is fashionable for both sexes and people often use cosmetics to darken their skin. But the ancient and modern fashions are really very similar in their explanation. Nowadays, in industrialized societies, most ordinary people are pale through working indoors in factories and offices. So, having a suntan suggests that a person is more prosperous than most and can afford to take long holidays in the sun. For us, as for the ancient Greeks, complexion is a badge of wealth.

For many Greek women there was another important reason for staying indoors: that was where their male relatives wanted them to be. If a married woman went out often, she might fall in love with a man other than her husband. A girl might find a boyfriend of whom her father disapproved. One Athenian wrote that a woman should not go out until she was old enough to have grown-up children. He thought that by then she would be too old to appeal to most men. A young woman was not even supposed to open the outer door of a house in case she came face to face with a man. But Greek writers often describe women as "peeping out" of their houses.

What did a woman do indoors? If she belonged to a wealthy family she supervised her slaves while they did the household tasks. There would then be much time for her to chat to female relatives. One man complained about prosperous women who "sat around grandly" doing nothing. But most women did their own cooking and cleaning—though not shopping. (Men and slaves did that.)

Women brought up their sons until they were old enough for school. Daughters usually did not go to school; they learned to run a house by helping their mother at home. Some girls were

One male poet complained that a few women were too grand to sit by an oven and get themselves dirty. But most women had to sweat over the cooking.

Spinning was a familiar task for Greek women whether they were slaves or citizen-wives.

taught to read and write, perhaps by their mothers, but men might object to this. A literate female had too much power! One male character in a comedy says:

"Teach a woman letters? A serious mistake! Like giving extra poison to a terrifying snake."

Even prosperous women were allowed to go outdoors sometimes. Religious festivals were occasions for meeting, talking, and showing off fine clothes and jewellery. Family occasions, such as the birth of a child or a funeral, also brought women together.

The majority of citizen women were poor. For them, going out to work was often a necessity. Women would join the men to work in the fields at harvest time, as many still do in Greece today. They also sold food and clothing in the market. And, if a woman had had a child, she could earn money by being a wet-nurse—that is, by suckling another woman's baby.

Educated women

Some women from eastern Greece were able to get a superior education. Thargelia of Miletos, for example, was thought to be a political agent for the king of Persia. Aspasia, also of Miletos, was famous for her brains. She lived with Perikles, the great politician of Athens.

More famous still was Sappho. She was a poet in the early 500s BC and lived on the isle of Lesbos. She wrote in a clear and simple style, often about the people she loved:

"I have a beautiful daughter, who looks like the golden flowers, my beautiful Kleis: I would not exchange her for all the kingdom of Lydia..."

"Love has shaken my heart, like a wind falling on the oaks of the mountainside."

Sappho and her poems reflect love and jealousy between women on the island of Lesbos.

Colonization and Trade

Greece is not by nature a rich country, as we have seen. Much of its land is bare mountain; water is often scarce and the soil shallow. When faced with serious shortages, Greeks often chose one of two solutions. They either emigrated to a richer territory and lived together as a colony, or they traded and brought home what they needed by sea.

A map of Greek towns in the 400s BC shows settlements stretching far beyond the area of mainland Greece. Towns were scattered from the Black Sea coast in the east to Spain in the west.

Colonization took place in waves. The western coast of Asia Minor was settled soon after the fall of Mycenae (see page 28). Later, in the 700s-500s BC, countless other colonies were founded, especially around the Black Sea and western Mediterranean. Corinth created two of the most important ones: Kerkyra (Corfu) and Syracuse. The little state of Phokaia founded Massalia (now Marseilles) in southern Gaul, and Massalia founded Nikaia (Nice). Miletos in Ionia, once a colony itself, set up over 70 colonies near the Black Sea.

Sometimes colonists were unwilling to leave home. The historian Herodotos tells of men from the isle of Thera setting off to colonize north Africa. The colonists lost heart and sailed back to Thera. But the people at home gave them an angry reception. They threw things at the boats and would not let the men land. They were forced to return to Africa, where they founded the colony of Cyrene. It was probably a shortage of resources that forced Thera to send some of its people away in the first place.

The colonies around the Mediterranean did not form an empire. Greek settlers usually stayed on or near the coast; they often traded with their independent non-Greek neighbours by land and with other Greeks by sea.

Greek cities and their colonies were sprinkled over a vast area. It took courage—or desperation—to leave home, sail for weeks, then settle on an unknown coast, as the colonists did.

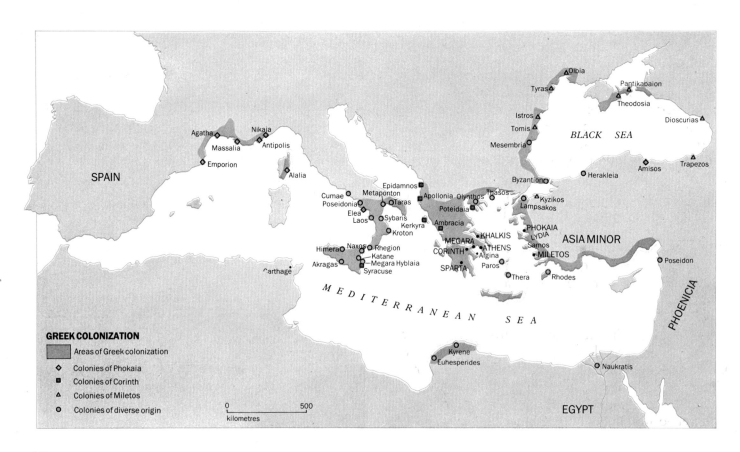

GREEK COLONIZATION

- Areas of Greek colonization
- ◇ Colonies of Phokaia
- ■ Colonies of Corinth
- △ Colonies of Miletos
- ○ Colonies of diverse origin

0   500
kilometres

A vase in the shape of a black person's head—evidence of Greek trade with Africa.

Exports and imports

What did Greek traders carry in their ships? For Athens and other states a vital import was grain, which came mainly from lands north of the Black Sea. In exchange, Athens sent silver from her mines. Olive oil and wine were exported, and so was pottery from Corinth and Athens. (Many fine Athenian vases have been found in northern Italy, where wealthy non-Greeks treasured them.)

Greece is short of trees, so naval powers such as Corinth, Aigina and Athens imported timber for shipbuilding. Most of it came from lands north of the Aegean. Salted fish was also imported; luxurious fabrics and dyes came from Phoenicia and Carthage, and papyrus to write on came from Egypt. Many non-Greeks from the Mediterranean area were brought to serve as slaves.

Western Greeks

Greek colonies in Sicily and southern Italy were many and powerful. They are sometimes known by the Latin title of *Magna Graecia*—Great Greece. These colonies took part in the Olympic games, a badge of being Greek, and sometimes intervened in disputes on the Greek mainland.

The town of Sybaris in southern Italy became legendary for its wealth. Its wine was so plentiful that it ran in a canal, and, it was said, the wealthy citizens of Sybaris slept on beds of rose-petals. One Sybarite complained of the strain of seeing someone else work. The town was destroyed in war during the late 500s, but it had colonies of its own which lived on. One of these was Poseidonia (Paestum) where some fine temples survive (see page 10).

Coinage

Coinage seems to have been invented around 690 BC in the non-Greek kingdom of Lydia in western Asia Minor. It was not until the early 500s that the first Greek states started using coins for trade.

Aigina was among the first Greek cities to make coins. Aiginetan coinage showed a turtle. Athens' coins bore an owl (see page 47), symbol of "owl-eyed Athena". When Athens ruled the Aegean, she tried to prevent her subject states from making their own coins. Using "owls" became compulsory, which helped Athens' traders.

A merchant ship (left) and a warship. Life at sea was often uncomfortable and dangerous. Pirates came to be known as "drowners", drowning their victims was a way of preventing revenge—"dead men tell no tales". Probably the only time piracy was rare was during the 400s BC when Athens' warships ruled the Aegean.

The Army

During the Dark Age, cavalry probably dominated the battlefield. The speed of the horse made it possible for foot-soldiers to be attacked suddenly, even from a distance. Surprised and unprepared, they might well be terrified by horsemen pounding towards them. And if they fled they would easily be overtaken.

Rise of the hoplites

A technique was invented, however, which ended the rule of the horse, and made Greek infantry into the most feared land force of the eastern Mediterranean world. Around 700 BC, infantry learned to fight shoulder to shoulder and several ranks deep, in a body called a *phalanx*. Each man, known as a hoplite, protected his left side and his neighbour's right side with a strong round shield of wood and metal. He wore a metal helmet, with a crest to make him look taller. If he could afford it, he also wore a breastplate. He had a sword but usually he killed by jabbing a spear downwards at

Below left: A cavalryman, with spear, rides into battle. Below right: Greek armies often used non-Greek archers, like the one shown here with his eastern trousers.

an unprotected part of an enemy's body. This was commonly the neck, between breastplate and helmet.

Battle tactics

How did the phalanx manage to resist a cavalry charge? Horsemen at speed needed to be well spaced, to avoid colliding with each other. Hoplites, standing together, were much closer packed. So cavalry charging a phalanx would have faced an array of spears much denser than their own. Also, the horses themselves would have made large and easy targets. Much later, during the Middle Ages, war horses often had armour. But, to judge by their skeletons, horses of ancient Greece were probably too small to bear the combined weight of armour for themselves and of a heavily-armed rider.

Rival phalanxes clashed head on. How did one of them win? Every hoplite dreaded being at the end of his line with no comrade *on his right* to shelter him with a shield. So, as the enemy approached, the man at the end often moved away to his right to avoid the coming clash. His neighbour followed him, to keep the protection of the first man's shield, and so on until the whole line had shifted to the right. Each army might thus

have an overlapping right wing. Each right wing could then try to go round the enemy's flank, to attack from the unguarded rear.

By better fighting, or by having a larger army which pushed harder, one phalanx might break through the other. This would leave at least one soldier in the broken phalanx at the end of a line, with no one's shield to guard his right side. But he could not solve his problem by moving to the right because the enemy was there. So he might well turn and run, leaving the man on his left in the position of danger. He too might run, and so on until much of the phalanx was in retreat.

When hoplites fled in disorder, they lost their power and became very easy to attack. They moved slowly in their heavy armour and their shields could not protect their backs. Enemy cavalry caught them: attacking small groups of hoplites from behind, the horsemen no longer faced a thicket of spears. Also, hoplites running with their backs to the enemy could not watch their opponents properly.

A beaten hoplite often threw away his heavy shield, to run faster. So, if he came home without his shield, a hoplite might be treated as a coward. If he came home with no blood on his weapons, it seemed he had been avoiding the fighting. Some unsuccessful hoplites dipped their spears in the bodies of men that others had killed. Then they had some blood to impress the people at home.

Two hoplite phalanxes clash. It was vital to keep the wall of shields unbroken. Notice the double support of the shield: a loop for the forearm and a handle behind the rim.

City States

The Greek world was made up of hundreds of independent city states. Many of them were tiny, with only a few hundred male citizens each. In other words, it was common for a self-governing state in Greece to have fewer people than many schools today have pupils. Athens in the Classical period had by far the largest population—about 250,000. But even that is small by the standards of modern cities.

A Greek state was called a *polis*. (From this come many modern words, such as "politics", "police" and "policy".) Each state had its own customs, festivals and form of government. For example, classical Athens was ruled by general meetings, in which the poor had great power. Megara, a few miles down the road, was ruled for many years by an oligarchy—a small group of wealthy men.

A *polis* might also use a different dialect of Greek from its neighbours. In the Athenian dialect, for example, the phrase meaning "to the city" was *eis ten polin*. But Megarians said *es tan polin*. (Megarians founded the colony of Byzantion. Their phrase *es tan polin* may be the origin of Byzantion's present name, Istanbul.)

Disputes between city states

There was almost ceaseless war, or fear of war, between many *poleis*. If you conquered another *polis* you freed yourself of the fear that it would attack you. But because the conquest made you more powerful, other states became afraid of *you* and therefore more likely to form an alliance to make war on you.

The most powerful city states of the Classical period were Athens and Sparta and each gained an empire over other *poleis*. But each found that large numbers of other Greeks joined forces to resist its empire. On the other hand, when a state was unusually weak, as a result of war or disease, hostile neighbours sometimes seized the opportunity to attack.

It was common for a *polis* to surround itself with a defensive wall of stone. Often this was built around a rocky hill, an *akropolis* ("high city"). The rock would prevent a besieging enemy from digging under the wall, and the slopes would allow boulders to be rolled down against attackers.

The chief cities of the Greek world, after the main waves of colonization had ended.

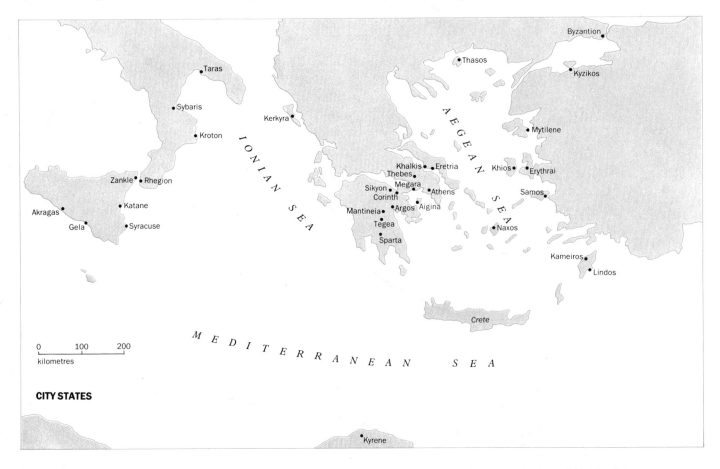

CITY STATES

Sparta

Sparta was unlike other Greek states; its male citizens were full-time soldiers. Though few, they became the terror of the Greek world.

The Spartans had made many neighbouring Greeks work for them as serfs, or "helots". They knew that the helots hated Sparta and would gladly "eat Spartans raw". Also, there were far more helots than Spartans. So, to keep the helots obediently at work, Spartan men made themselves into ferociously efficient warriors.

It was dangerous for citizens of Sparta to quarrel. That might encourage helots to attack. So Spartans were trained to think alike. Boys all had the same education and shared a life in barracks. Also, any drunkenness would make it easier for helots to attack. So, no *symposia* at Sparta, and no drunken guests wandering noisily home by torchlight. Instead, Spartans were trained to move stealthily at night, without lights, cutting the throats of unruly helots.

From time to time the Spartans ordered all other Greeks to leave the city. This may have been to allow Spartan soldiers to develop new military strategies, and to keep secret the size of its army. For the population of Sparta was far smaller than that of many rival states. Cunning had to make up for numbers.

Spartan girls wrestled and ran races. Their short tunics horrified other Greeks, who believed citizen women should be modestly dressed. This statuette probably shows a Spartan girl athlete.

The Spartan hoplites were well trained, ferocious fighters. Sometimes an enemy would turn and run at the mere sight of Spartan shields. (The upturned V was "L"—for "Lakedaimon", Sparta's usual name.)

Tyrants Take Power

We saw earlier (page 42) how the coming of the hoplite phalanx reduced the power of the aristocrats and their cavalry. The fairly prosperous men who served as hoplites grew in confidence and power, and soon rulers appeared to champion them against the aristocrats. These new rulers of the Greek cities were known as *tyrants*.

Greeks remembered the later tyrants with distaste and gave their name the unfavourable sense it still has. But early tyrants were treated as saviours.

In Corinth, Kypselos became tyrant, overthrowing the old aristocracy of the Bakkhiads. A tale came to be told about him, rather like the later story about Christ. It was said that, at the time of Kypselos' birth, his rule had already been prophesied. The Bakkhiads were afraid and, like King Herod in the Bible, tried to kill the baby. But the infant Kypselos smiled at the would-be murderers and they could not bear to kill him.

This story shows that Kypselos was once very popular. If he had not been, people would not have told a story of him as a smiling baby. Kypselos probably earned popularity by distributing the wealth of the Bakkhiads.

Greek tyrants often came to a nasty end, like the murder shown above. Their killers were citizens avenging insults from the tyrant or his friends.

The tyrants of Athens built many fine structures, such as the ornamented spring-house shown below.

The Rise of Athens

In the 500s BC Athens laid the foundations of its greatness. It was about to become the main rival of Sparta, and perhaps the most successful state ever in the production and development of ideas.

One great asset of the Athenians was their gentleness in internal politics. Other large states, such as Argos and Kerkyra, spent much of their energy in savage internal conflict. Athens, too, had tensions between rich and poor but these were handled more intelligently. As a result, Athens had the energy to expand overseas and the peaceful leisure for creative life at home.

In the early 500s many Athenians were protesting bitterly about the rich. The poor, they said, were losing their land to the rich and were being sold by them into slavery. But the Athenians managed to agree in choosing a man to settle the quarrel—Solon. He rescued many from slavery and protected the poor's future interests. But he refused to become a tyrant or to attack the rich. By not shedding blood he prevented the creation of a long-lasting feud between rich and poor.

Some resentment remained, however, and Peisistratos was made tyrant in 546 BC. Though he

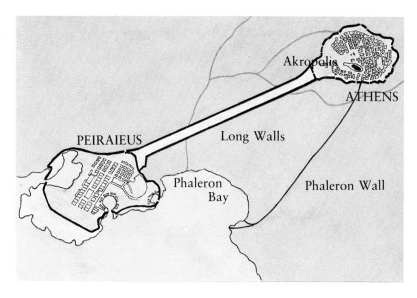

In the 450s BC long walls were built, linking the city of Athens with its port, the Peiraieus. From then on, the land army of Athens' enemy, Sparta, could not encircle and cut off the city. Athens' fleet brought supplies to the Peiraieus, and from there they were taken safely to the city, along the corridor formed by the long walls.

The best-known type of coin in the Greek world—the "owl", issued by Athens. It symbolized the owl-eyed goddess, Athena.

behaved mildly to the rich, his sons were less enlightened. One, disappointed in love, reacted by insulting his beloved's sister. For this he was assassinated. His brother, the tyrant Hippias, killed many citizens out of fear for himself. He was removed in 510 BC and the tyranny ended.

But the age of tyrants saw much prosperity in Athens. Athenian painted pottery, first the black-figure and then the red-, became the most successful in the Greek world. And, like tyrants elsewhere, Peisistratos' family created fine public buildings.

Athens' wealth

Athens had two great natural assets: a silver mine at Laureion and a superb harbour, the Peiraieus. The brilliant politician, Themistokles, saw how to use both.

In the 480s BC Laureion was found to be far richer than had been thought. Should the extra silver simply be distributed among the citizens? Themistokles thought not. He persuaded the Athenians to build a fleet with the money. This fleet defeated the Persians and, based at Peiraieus, was then used to found Athens' empire.

The Persian Wars

By 500 BC the Middle East was a Persian empire. Darius the Great, King of Persia, ruled the coastal lands of the eastern Mediterranean from Thrace and Asia Minor to Egypt and Libya. His empire also stretched eastwards to the borders of Russia and India.

In the 490s, some Greek towns revolted against this colossal power. Led by the town of Miletos, home of energetic colonizers and thinkers, Ionian Greeks of coastal Asia Minor stood against Darius, and were crushed. Athenians had come from the independent Greek mainland to help the rebels. Darius remembered.

In 490 he sent an army across the Aegean Sea to punish Athens. But his men were defeated on the plain of Marathon. (A legend later grew up that a runner carried news of the victory to Athens—the first Marathon run.)

The defeat had to be avenged. Otherwise Persia's subjects would think it weak and might revolt. Darius's son, King Xerxes, assembled a huge force to conquer Greece. He commanded it himself. His engineers made a bridge of boats at the stretch of water called the Hellespont: the great army marched across the sea. To protect his ships as they escorted the army westwards, Xerxes had a canal dug through a peninsula: the fleet sailed across the land.

Faced with this terrifying threat, the Greek

Persian troops, having climbed a precipice, capture the Akropolis of Athens. Desperate Athenians jump to their deaths.

CITY STATES

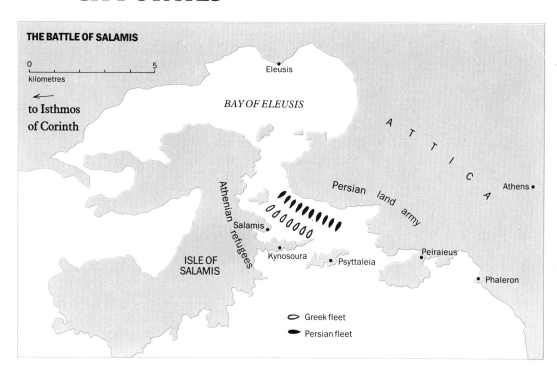

THE BATTLE OF SALAMIS

0 — 5 kilometres

to Isthmos of Corinth

BAY OF ELEUSIS

Eleusis

ATTICA

Athens

Persian land army

Athenian refugees

Salamis

ISLE OF SALAMIS

Kynosoura

Psyttaleia

Peiraieus

Phaleron

○ Greek fleet
● Persian fleet

The battle of Salamis in 480 BC probably saved Greece from permanent Persian rule. The promise of an easy victory lured the Persians into the Salamis strait. But in the strait they could not use their huge fleet to encircle the Greek ships. The slower, stronger, Greek vessels ground them down in a crowded battle.

commanders kept their wits. They calculated that they should fight the Persians in narrow spaces. This would prevent the enemy from using its vast numbers to encircle and trap the Greek forces.

Persian successes

The Greeks made their first stand at Thermopylai in 480 BC. Here a small force, led by Sparta, blocked a narrow pass between mountains and sea. Alongside, the Greek fleet blocked a narrow channel. But some Persian troops used a mountain track to appear *behind* the Greek foot-soldiers. Trapped between two enemy forces, the 300 Spartans, with their allies, died fighting. For Persia, the road to central Greece and Athens now lay open.

A few Athenians stayed on their Akropolis, defiantly rolling down boulders against the might of the Persian empire. But the enemy unexpectedly scaled a precipice to reach the top of the citadel. The defenders were slaughtered, some jumping to their deaths on the rocks far below. Most Athenians, however, had already left, choosing to resist by sea. Apollo's oracle at Delphi had prophesied that the city of Athens would be captured. Only a "wooden wall" would survive.

Athens wins at sea

The "wooden wall" seemed to mean the wooden warships of Athens. The Athenians wanted a sea-

battle near their city, in the narrow channel between the mainland and the isle of Salamis. Other Greeks refused at first, but they gave in when Athens threatened that its vital fleet might sail away and leave them.

Themistokles, Athens' general, tricked the Persians into attacking in the narrows of Salamis. He seems to have sent a secret message to Xerxes, saying that the Greeks were quarrelling and would scarcely resist if attacked immediately. The enemy did attack—just as the Greeks wanted.

The stronger, heavier Greek warships rammed and shattered the Persian vessels in the crowded narrows. (The nimbler enemy ships might have fought far better in the open sea, with space to manoeuvre.) An Athenian poet later described the blood in the sea from Xerxes' shipwrecked sailors, speared like fish. The Persian king watched from a nearby hill. Defeated, he turned for home.

Much of the Persians' land army remained. But in the next year, 479 BC, it too was defeated—at Plataia, north-west of Athens. The Greek hoplites, led by Sparta, proved too much for their more lightly equipped enemy. Other Greeks sailed east and defeated a Persian force in Asia Minor, near Mykale.

The great Persian threat was now removed. We shall see next how Athens used the victory—and what might have happened to Athens, and Greek civilization, if Persia had won.

49

Classical Greece
Athens Rules the Waves

The Persians never invaded Greece again. King Xerxes got home safely but later was murdered. Athens was left free to develop the ideas and art which made it famous, and which have influenced other civilizations ever since. But if the Persians had conquered Greece, things would have been very different. The earlier fate of Miletos shows what might well have happened.

Miletos had been the first capital of the new Greek way of life. But, after failing in the Ionian revolt of the 490s BC, the city was captured by the Persians and crippled for ever. Many of its women were "snatched away to the King of Persia". Only fragments now remain of the works of Milesian thinkers. Without the victories of Salamis and Plataia, Athens might have been crushed even more thoroughly.

Athens forms an alliance
When the victorious Athenians returned to their city, what they found made them very angry. The Persians had wrecked it. Families had lost their homes and the temples were destroyed. Athens looked for revenge.

Sparta was not very interested in carrying on the war, once the main Persian forces had left. But Athens was keen. Its large fleet was well suited to war against a distant enemy, and eastern Greeks turned to Athens for leadership. A new alliance was formed. It pledged to free eastern Greeks still under Persian control and to take revenge for Xerxes' invasion by raiding the Persian empire.

The fight was hard and long. We hear of one brave Persian commander, Boges, who defended a fort on the northern coast of the Aegean. When,

after a long siege, he saw that the Greeks were bound to capture the fort, he threw all his treasure into a nearby river. He had his wife and mistresses put to death, and then killed himself.

The alliance becomes an empire

As fear of Persia faded, some of the allies lost interest in the hard task of chipping away at the Persian empire. They refused to fight or to send money for the campaigns. But Athens would not let them drop out in this way. It probably argued that dropping out would let down the other Greeks and help the Persians. So Athens sent its warships against these former allies and forced them to continue making payments. Then, in the mid 450s, the treasury of the alliance was moved to Athens.

Athens now controlled the alliance's money. Many of the allies even fought for Athens in a war against Sparta. The alliance had become an Athenian empire.

Left: An Athenian trireme brings instructions to Samos, an important subject state of the empire. The merchant ships have brought things to sell. Below: Athena clasps the hand of Hera, goddess of Samos. Samians were made citizens of Athens as a reward for their loyalty in war.

But by now both Athens and Persia had had enough of war. From 448 BC the Athenians felt free to spend the allies' treasure on a peaceful project—the creation of superb buildings for Athens itself.

The empire was used to fulfil the dreams of ordinary Athenians. They wanted land—they got it by confiscating estates of rich men in the empire. They wanted wages—they got them from service in the fleet and on building projects. Food became more plentiful, because Athenian warships were able to guard merchant vessels bringing grain from southern Russia. The Athenian fleet also prevented other states from competing to buy the grain. As a result, Athenian merchants bought it more cheaply.

One wealthy poet teased the ordinary people of Athens. He joked that they dreamed of conquering Persia, then of sitting at the heart of Persian territory making easy money and eating sweets. But rich men, too, profited from the Athenian empire. Thucydides of Athens, probably the finest historian of the ancient world, owned a gold mine which the Athenian fleet protected. This gave him the leisure to write.

Another poet listed some of the fine cargoes brought to Athens at this time. They included leather from Cyrene, salted fish from the Hellespont, beef from Italy, sails and rope from Egypt, incense from Syria, ivory from Libya, carpets and elegant cushions from Carthage, dates and flour from Phoenicia. (We notice that many of the places named were within the Persian empire.)

In states of the Athenian empire, rich and poor frequently clashed. Athens sided with the poor. It removed many of the rich—the oligarchs—from power, and set up *demokratia*. This gave ordinary people more influence and dignity by involving them in decision-making.

When Sparta was at war with Athens during the late 400s, rich men were encouraged to rebel against the Athenians. Many of these rebels were caught and executed by Athens. But ordinary people in towns that formed part of the Athenian empire were reluctant to lose its support. Without the protection of Athens, well-known supporters of the *demokratia* might be massacred by the oligarchs or by Sparta.

Building the Parthenon

When the long wars against Persia came to an end, the Athenians wanted to celebrate. They were safe, they had won great victories over a terrifying opponent, and they had gained an empire. They were very proud of themselves. And they were grateful to Athena, the patron goddess of their city. She represented not only Athens but also warfare and intelligence.

A reward for Athena

During the Persian invasion, Athena was thought to have given wise advice on strategy. A sacred snake, believed to be connected with Athena, had left the Akropolis as the Persians approached. This was taken as a sign from the goddess that she herself had departed, and that the Athenians should follow her—to fight not on the Akropolis but at sea. For showing them the correct strategy, Athena deserved a great reward. She was to be given a temple of outstanding lavishness and beauty—the Parthenon (see pages 54–55).

Work on the new building began in 447 BC,
funded by the treasure received from Athens' allies. The site of the temple was the finest in the city: the central section of the Akropolis. There were magnificent views up there for the goddess to enjoy—over Athenian territory and out across the Aegean Sea.

The architect, Iktinos, designed the columns of the new temple to taper slightly at the top. If they had been built perfectly straight, optical illusion might have made them seem too thin in the middle. Other slight curves were built into the base of the temple so that it would appear light and graceful.

Working with Iktinos was the sculptor Pheidias, most of whose work can still be seen. In the gables, the high triangular sections at each end of the temple, Pheidias designed scenes involving Athena. One showed her birth: according to legend she sprang fully formed from the head of Zeus. The other scene showed Athena creating an olive tree in Athenian soil, from which was to grow the city's great industry of olive-oil production. Slightly lower on the building were sculptures showing the defeat of the centaurs—monsters, half man and half horse. These were probably to remind people of the defeat of the monstrous Persians. And around the inner section of the temple, just below its ceiling, was a stone frieze. It showed the *Panathenaia*—the city's procession in honour of Athena.

But Pheidias's greatest work, the centrepiece of the whole project, was the statue of Athena Parthenos ("the Virgin") to stand inside the main chamber of the temple. It was about 13 metres high and showed the goddess with the sacred snake beside her shield. The clothing on the statue was of gold. (Pheidias made it in separate plates—easily taken off and weighed—so that people could tell he had not been stealing.) Since Athena

The Akropolis ("High City") of Athens, crowned by the ruin of the Parthenon. To the left, on the shoulder of the Akropolis, is the gateway complex, the Propylaia. The theatre below the hill was built by a Roman who admired Athens, Herodes Atticus.

was noble, her flesh had to be gleaming white. Pheidias made it of ivory. Sadly, but not surprisingly, this statue with its precious materials disappeared long ago.

The finished temple glittered. Its freshly-cut marble was brilliant white. Much of the sculpture was brightly painted in reds and blues. Shimmering outside, in the intense Greek sunlight, was another great statue—of Athena Promakhos ("the Defender"). Sailors could see it from far out at sea.

The temple brings prosperity

Today people see the Parthenon as one of the most beautiful and important buildings ever made. Looking at it they think of the intelligence and creativity of the Greeks. But some Athenians of the time thought the temple a dreadful, undignified thing.

The politician who championed the proposal to build the Parthenon was Perikles. He was an aristocrat but he aimed to please the majority of Athenian citizens, who were poor. Perikles knew that building the temple would bring wages to many of these ordinary citizens. For instance, quarrymen would cut out the blocks of marble; carters would transport the stone to the Akropolis; cart-makers and breeders of oxen would supply the means of transport; sculptors, masons, carpenters and countless other craftsmen and labourers would build the temple itself. And when they spent their money in Athens, almost the whole city would benefit. In addition, everyone would know that the money came from Athens' empire, and this would make them proud.

Opposition to the Parthenon

Opponents of Perikles quietly dreaded this. They were rich men who did not really approve of *demokratia*—the rule of the poor. *They* wanted to be seen as the people who paid for expensive public buildings, because that would make them well-known and win them political support. They did not want the people of Athens to depend on, and support, the empire, because the empire promoted *demokratia*. But Perikles' opponents probably did not say all this publicly; that would have made them unpopular. Instead, they said that the Parthenon would be a huge waste of money and would make Athens like a deceitful woman. What did they mean?

When a Greek woman beautified herself she

Part of the Parthenon frieze, showing horsemen on their way to the Akropolis. You can still see the holes in the horses, drilled by Pheidias's men, to which bridles made of bronze were attached. In other parts of the frieze, animals are brought for sacrifice, girls carry sacred vessels, and men ride in chariots.

often put on built-up shoes to make herself look taller. She dabbed red make-up on her cheeks and put white powder on the rest of her face. The aim was to make herself look wealthier than she really was. (Women of wealthy family were probably taller than most, because of a better diet during childhood. And, as we have seen, they were pale from spending much of their time indoors.)

We can now see how the opponents of the Parthenon could compare Athens to a deceitful woman. The Parthenon made the Akropolis a little taller (as built-up shoes did to a woman). Small sculpted sections of the new building were painted bright red (like parts of a woman's cheeks). And most of the remaining stonework was brilliant white, like the powder on a woman's face. Also, like a beautified woman, the Parthenon falsely suggested wealth. Other Greeks might say: "How much money Athens must have, if it can afford to lavish so much on a temple." But Perikles was probably happy for the temple to deceive other Greek states in this way. If they overestimated the wealth of Athens, they might be more afraid to make war against it.

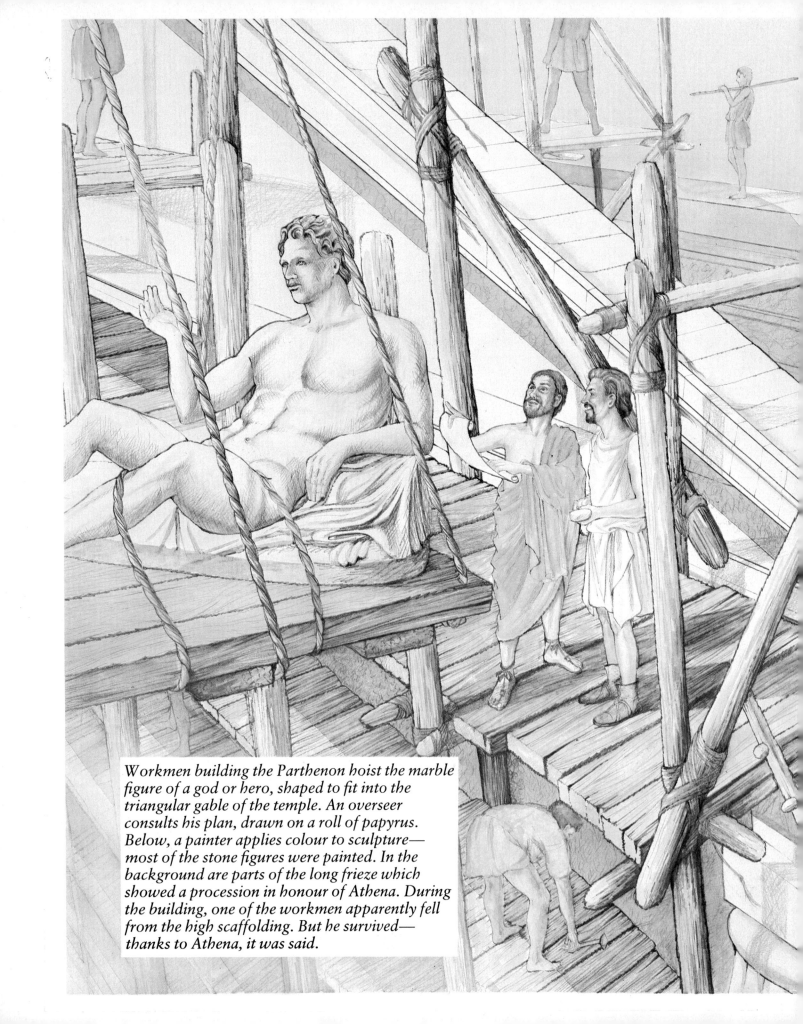

Workmen building the Parthenon hoist the marble figure of a god or hero, shaped to fit into the triangular gable of the temple. An overseer consults his plan, drawn on a roll of papyrus. Below, a painter applies colour to sculpture—most of the stone figures were painted. In the background are parts of the long frieze which showed a procession in honour of Athena. During the building, one of the workmen apparently fell from the high scaffolding. But he survived—thanks to Athena, it was said.

Demokratia

Many modern states are called democracies. But their forms of government are very different from the *demokratia* of the Greeks. The Greek system was easier to understand and, if you were a man, more fun to take part in.

Of all the Greek states which had *demokratia*, Athens is by far the best known. In the 400s BC it set up and protected *demokratia* in other states. The Spartans, who feared and hated this form of government, knew it was Athens above all which they had to attack.

Athenians in their assembly, the most famous and sophisticated democratic body of the ancient world. The hill behind the speaker is the Pynx. Slave archers, in caps, keep order.

Demokratia meant government by mass meeting. At Athens a general assembly was held on average once in nine days and every ordinary male citizen was free to attend, speak and vote. In practice, normal attendance at an assembly was about five to six thousand. The city was governed by the votes of this crowd. Did the system work?

The general assembly

The general assembly was often noisy and exciting. Rival speakers taunted each other, and the crowd enjoyed seeing a boastful speaker coming to grief. In 425 BC the assembly discussed how to capture some Spartans who had occupied the island of Sphakteria. A politician named Kleon said that the generals were not real men. If he, Kleon, were general, the Athenians would have more success against the Spartans. "Well then," said Nikias, who was one of the generals, "we'll

put you in command. See if *you* can do better at Sphakteria." "Right," said Kleon, thinking that Nikias was not serious. But he soon realized that Nikias *was* serious and that he might have to live up to his boast. This frightened him and he tried to take back his words. But the more he tried, the more the crowd shouted at him to accept the command and, in the end, he had to agree. (For how well he did, see page 79.)

This is probably the best-known of the debates at the assembly. It shows Athenians making a serious decision in a rather light-hearted way. We know the details of this debate because it was recorded by Thucydides. But Thucydides was an enemy of Kleon and disapproved of *demokratia*. He was perhaps using the debate to persuade his readers that they too should disapprove. Other debates, which Thucydides did not describe, must have been treated more seriously by the assembly. Otherwise the Athenians could hardly have won and kept an empire.

Oligarchies

During the Classical period, the usual alternative to *demokratia* was *oligarkhia*—rule by a few unelected, rich men. Under this system, ordinary people were often treated harshly because they lacked the power to defend themselves. Hatred resulted. The philosopher Plato said that a city with an oligarchy was really two cities—a city of the rich and a city of the poor—each plotting against the other. We even hear that some oligarchs swore a solemn oath to "do as much damage to the pro-democratic masses as they could". A city so divided could hardly work efficiently. Much of its energy would be spent on internal strife. In contrast, under the *demokratia* of Athens, rich and poor seem usually to have tolerated each other, each feeling they had a fair degree of control over decisions.

People living under a Greek oligarchy (like people in a modern democracy) must often have been surprised by government decisions. They

Ostraka (left), with the names of Athenian politicians whom the voters wanted to be sent into exile, or ostracized. On the right are metal voting disks for the lawcourts. The one on the left meant "not guilty", the one on the right meant "guilty".

could even wake up to find themselves suddenly at war, because overnight the government had so decided. But ordinary Athenians would have said, "War? Impossible. We didn't vote for one!"

In other words, *demokratia* made fairly sure that the important decisions, such as when to go to war, reflected what most men wanted. Although women and slaves could not take part in general assemblies, ordinary men had more power than is usual in countries today.

Ostracism

To make a long speech to the crowded assembly needed courage. It seems that few ordinary Athenians became well-known speakers. They may have lacked self-confidence and preferred to leave speech-making to better-educated men—which, in practice, meant the rich. Many of Athens' great leaders were aristocrats (Perikles is the most famous.) But they did not form a government – their ideas were only adopted if they persuaded the assembly. And the assembly was dominated by the votes of ordinary citizens. Even Perikles' advice was sometimes rejected by the assembly.

In the crowd at each assembly there would always be some citizens who had not been at the previous assembly. So there was always a risk that an assembly might make plans which conflicted with the ideas of the earlier meeting. The risk was especially great if there were two very persuasive speakers who were rivals. One speaker might persuade an assembly to do one thing; then, a few days later, his rival might persuade another assembly to do the opposite. To prevent this happening, the Athenians invented *ostracism*. Citizens took a vote between the rival politicians. The loser had to go into exile for ten years.

Officials chosen by lottery

In the *demokratia* of Athens elections were treated with suspicion. Every year ten men were elected as generals. But the Athenians knew that election favoured men from well-known families—aristocrats and the rich. So most of their officials were chosen by a method which seemed more democratic—lottery.

Everyone had an equal chance in a lottery. As a result, most of the officials chosen by lottery were ordinary men with little money. The Athenians knew that these people were not as well educated

Speakers in Athenian lawcourts were given a fixed time for their speeches, as in the United States Supreme Court today. Clockwork was unknown, so time was measured by water. The plug was pulled out of the top jar so that the water slowly ran out into the jar below. When the top jar was empty, the speaker had to finish his speech.

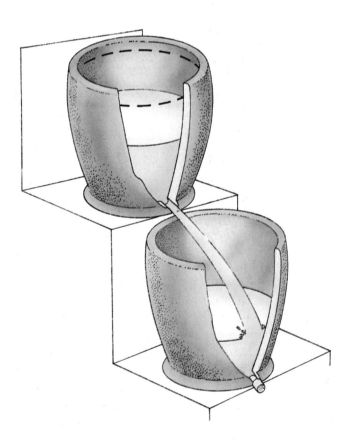

as the rich. But they thought that these officials would know more, and care more, about ordinary people's problems, because they themselves were ordinary people.

The council

When the general assembly met, its time was precious. Thousands of citizens attended. There was a risk that a few people would make silly suggestions and that the time of the thousands would be wasted in discussing them. So, before a proposal could be made in the assembly, it had to be approved by a smaller group, the council.

There were 500 council members, all chosen by lot. They were given pay, because without it many of the poorer citizens could not have taken part. But no one could be a council member for more than two years of his life. The Athenians did not want permanent officials who might lose touch with ordinary life.

The council met almost every day. Urgent news was brought to it. For example, when the frightening message arrived that King Philip of Macedon was approaching Athens with a hostile army, it was the council that received the news. It then called an assembly to decide what to do.

Law and order

Lottery was also used to pick the juries for legal cases. Juries were much larger than those of today and sometimes thousands of jurors heard an important case. A large jury like this would be sure to contain many ordinary people. It would also be very difficult for a rich man to bribe it!

A large jury behaved rather like the crowd at an assembly. The jurors called out questions during the prosecutor's and defendant's speeches. They also made a din to show when they approved or disapproved of what was being said.

Some cases were dramatic. On one occasion a prosecutor tried to make money unfairly; he accused someone of murdering a woman and hiding her body. But the defendant argued in court that the woman was not dead at all and that the prosecutor himself had been hiding her. To prove his story he brought the woman, alive and well, into court. When the jurors took their usual vote at the end of the trial, not one voted for the prosecutor. So he was fined for bringing a wrongful prosecution.

Slaves

At Athens, much of the hard and dirty work was done by slaves. Some of these unfree people were Greeks, but most were from the non-Greek lands around the eastern Mediterranean.

Not all slaves were treated the same. Some even had a little power over citizens, such as the archers from Skythia (southern Russia) who kept order in the Athenian assembly. Good-looking female slaves were often trained to be entertainers. They had to work with enthusiasm and a smile at parties, and were no doubt given friendly treatment to keep the atmosphere pleasant. Sometimes one of these women pleased a man so much that he paid for her to be freed. And some of the cleverer male slaves were allowed to work on their own, keeping part of the profit they made. Several slaves became bankers and bought their own freedom with their savings.

Such slaves, however, were few. We can tell how most slaves lived from Aristotle's idea that slaves in general were physically stronger than free men and walked less uprightly. This suggests that slaves had to do much heavy labour, which developed their muscles. They may have walked with a stoop because they were used to carrying heavy loads. Or they may have kept their heads

A trained woman slave helps a citizen home from a party. He has had too much to drink!

Drink is lowered to slaves in a mine. Dangerous, and with cruel overseers, a mine was one of the worst places to work.

down from modesty and to protect themselves from contemptuous looks.

Slaves did much of the housework. It was because slaves ran errands and fetched water that wealthy women were able to stay indoors, keeping their skin pale. In the countryside, farms were run by slave labour.

In one short period from 413 BC, over 20,000 slaves ran away from their Athenian owners. They fled to a base which Sparta had set up near Athens. This large number suggests that there may have been more slaves than citizens. It also suggests that the slaves were very unhappy, because running away to the Spartans was itself a very dangerous thing to do. Sparta was famous for its ill-treatment of slaves.

It may help us to understand the Athenian treatment of slaves if we think of our own treatment of animals today. In public, people are ashamed to mistreat their pets or farm animals, but in private things may be very different. At Athens it was thought wrong to humiliate or beat slaves in public. But one poet joked cruelly that slaves (in private) got so many beatings that in the end they did not notice the blows. Slaves far from public view, in the mines or on remote farms, probably had the worst treatment.

Town Life

If we were suddenly transported back in time to a street in ancient Athens or Corinth, we should immediately notice two things. One would be the noise. There were no cars, road drills or other motor-driven machinery, so the main sound in a town was the human voice. A joke was told about the luxury-loving men of Sybaris who liked to spend their nights at parties. To allow themselves to sleep peacefully during the day, they banned all noisy craftsmen. The joke may not be true but it reminds us that another common noise in a Greek town was the hammering of carpenters, cobblers and blacksmiths.

The other thing we should notice immediately would be the smell. The Greeks had no sewers. There were beetles which did the community an important service by eating dung—but they worked slowly!

In the warm climate of Greece, men spent much of their time in the streets. When they did their shopping they often carried small coins in the mouth, as people did in Dickens' London. One Greek poet joked about a man who got home to receive a warm kiss from his daughter. But then he noticed that the kiss was just an excuse. The girl's tongue was fishing out coins from his mouth.

Athens was rather different from many other Greek towns in the way people treated each other in the street. In many places it was normal for ordinary people to stand out of the way when a rich man approached. He would often have a group of friends and slaves around him, as he swept grandly along. But in Athens rich men complained that the poor would not make way for them. Plato, who disliked the Athenian *demokratia*, said that even donkeys and horses barged into people in Athens, as if they too felt they had democratic rights.

The picture shows a poor woman, a bread-seller, arguing with a man in expensive clothes. He has just collided with her and spoilt some of her goods. She is encouraged to stand up for herself by the knowledge that the Athenian courts will back her up, if necessary. The courts, as we have seen, were controlled by ordinary people and punished bad behaviour by the rich.

The two wealthy women to the left of the

A smith at his forge, working iron. The furnace made the smithy a favourite place for local people to chat on a cold day.

picture are escorting each other to an important family occasion—perhaps to see a new baby. Each shields her face from men's stares, by holding up her garment. (A painting on an Athenian vase shows us that women walked like this.) A girl from a poor family runs an errand on her own. Fetching water was one of the commonest jobs, because very few houses had their own supply.

Even in Greece, winters could make people miserably cold. For warmth, people gathered at bath houses or by the furnace at a blacksmith's forge. Most of the year men could sit and chat at barbers' shops, which were important places for passing on news and gossip. One Greek writer said that these gatherings at barbers' shops were really parties without wine. Young men also got free entertainment at the schools where attractive young women were trained to dance and play music.

At night a large town could be a dangerous place. There was no street lighting so men often carried blazing torches. (Indoors, people used little pottery oil lamps. These had a handle at one end and a lighted wick at the other.) Criminals lurked in the darkness. A common crime was to knock a man down and snatch his expensive cloak from his shoulders.

Family Life

Athens

In a wealthy family, husband and wife could live almost in different worlds. She stayed indoors, often with her daughters and other female relatives. He was outdoors, in the world of men. Neither did much housework or shopping. Those tasks were left to slaves. In a rich man's house there were separate quarters for the women, away from the men's area. One Athenian described an imaginary but realistic conversation between two wealthy men. One asks the other, "Is there anyone with whom you have fewer conversations than with your wife?" "Not many people, certainly", comes the reply.

Another reason for this separation of spouses was the difference in their ages. A girl usually married in her teens; her husband was often twice her age. They would have little in common at first so some young wives found themselves boyfriends nearer their own age. We hear of one husband who was put on trial for murder. He had come home unexpectedly, found his wife with a young man, and killed him.

For poorer, ordinary Athenians things were different. Poverty forced husband and wife together. There was not enough space in a small house to have separate quarters for men and women. Poor men did not have slaves, so their wives and children did the domestic work. Poor girls would also go outdoors on errands, which was something rich girls hardly ever did. This meant poor girls met more boys than rich girls did, and so probably married for love more often.

An Athenian speaker in court asked the men of the jury, "What would each of you say when you get home, and your wife or daughter asks, 'Where have you been?'. When you reply 'Judging a case', she will ask straightaway 'Who was on trial?'." This suggests that the jurors, who were mostly poor men, expected their female relatives to take an interest in what they had been doing. The speaker went on to warn the jurors not to take a decision in court which would anger the women. So it seems women did have some influence.

The birth of a child often made a husband and wife happier with each other. If the child was male, both parents could look forward to having someone to look after them in their old age. The wife could relax a little; there was now less chance of her husband divorcing her. (A divorced woman was all too often left isolated in Athenian society, especially if she was thought unable to have children.)

Sons often did not marry until they were well into their thirties; this could cause great domestic problems. There might be big lads around the house, wanting their independence, while their father wanted to go on dominating his family as he had in earlier years. Father and son often ended up fighting. Aristotle had a joke about a grown-up son who dragged his father to the door to throw him out. "Stop!" cried the father. "This is as far as I dragged *my* father!"

This sculpture, from a Greek colony in the western Mediterranean, shows a wealthy housewife storing some fabric in a chest. Wood for cupboards was scarce. Household implements hang on the walls.

Dirt and smells were a great nuisance in Greek houses. Here a baby is forced to use a potty to reduce the problem.

Sparta

Spartans seem to have had much less family life than ordinary Athenians. Sparta was rather like an army camp, as we have seen on page 45. Males, young and old, were meant to spend a lot of time together in large groups. In that way, it was hoped, they would grow to be similar in character, devoted to each other and ready to fight as a harmonious machine. Family life might spoil this. Different families might produce sons with conflicting ideas and characters. And men from happy families might be loyal to their relatives rather than to the community.

Small boys were taken from their families and put into groups for training. Girls may have been allowed to sleep at home, but they had to do outdoor exercises together. So they probably spent less time with their families than did most Athenian girls. Men were allowed to marry young but were not supposed to spend much time with their wives until they were thirty. So young married couples got together in secret.

The Spartans knew these secret meetings were taking place but they did not mind. In fact, they wanted them to take place. Sparta had a shortage of population, so husbands and wives had to be allowed to get together—for long enough to produce children. But if a young man spent very long with his wife, he might become more interested in her than in his fellow soldiers. Spartans did not marry in order to create close-knit families but to breed.

Spartan women, not seeing much of their men, were free to go out and spend time with each other. Other Greeks complained that the women of Sparta had too much freedom, and too much wealth. When Spartan men were away with the army, their wives were left to make important decisions for the community—something Athenians would probably never have allowed their women to do.

Spartan mothers had a reputation for being fierce towards their sons. A soldier who came home with no shield was thought to have thrown it away when fleeing as a coward. To come home carried on a shield meant that a man was dead. A Spartan mother is supposed to have sent her son away to war with the words: "Come home with a shield or on one." Meaning—but if you lose your shield, don't come back.

These little figures in clay show a favourite game for girls. The girls are throwing up and catching small animal bones.

Life in Sparta

The little community of Sparta had a serious problem: how to control the huge numbers of unfree people, the helots, who fed and clothed the Spartan citizens. Sparta thought up ways to solve its problem. They worked so well that for long Sparta was able to dominate not only the helots but much of the rest of Greece too.

The importance of unity

The Spartans realized that they must never split into rival groups. That would weaken the community and give the helots a chance to revolt. So, rich and poor citizens were not supposed to quarrel, as they did in other Greek states. Every night groups of male citizens, rich and poor together, ate the same simple food. Other Greeks said it tasted awful.

Spartans also understood the importance of education. To encourage male citizens to think and act in harmony, family life was largely abolished. Instead, all boys lived together and went to the same school. They were often whipped. This was to prepare them for pain and fear on the battlefield.

Boys and men were under constant pressure to live up to Sparta's strict military ideals. Boys had a competition to steal cheeses from an altar, while the defenders of the cheese tried to whip them. Late in Sparta's history some boys let themselves be whipped to death, to show their bravery.

Boys learned to travel in the dark, to steal food, to live in hunger and with few clothes. They might need these abilities as adults, when hunting rebel helots.

Young Spartans also learned to take orders from older boys. This would help them to be obedient soldiers later on—in a battle there was no time to argue. Obedience to elders was used, too, in the daily life of Sparta. Old men had great power, and more respect was shown to them than in other Greek towns. It suited Sparta to give power to the elderly because old men were not likely to have dangerous new ideas.

Teaching by example

Spartans were not encouraged to read books. These might teach revolutionary schemes from abroad, such as *demokratia*. Instead, Spartans taught their own people with real-life scenes.

The scene of the cheese-stealing contest was meant to teach watching boys to be brave. When Spartans were killed in battle, their relatives went round looking cheerful—to teach others that a brave death was a good thing. Helots, it seems, were sometimes forced to get drunk and to act in a ridiculous way. This scene was meant to teach Spartans to despise drunkenness and to see the danger of drinking wine. (This was important because if the Spartans themselves had got drunk, the helots could easily have overpowered them.)

Very many Spartans had 'horsey' names. The horse was vital for Spartan society. Only by riding could the citizens of Sparta patrol their large estates while still living together in Sparta itself. A Spartan high on his horse would enjoy feeling superior. And he would make a frightening sight for the helots, who went on foot.

Real-life images were also used against enemies. Spartan soldiers on the march wore red cloaks so that everyone would notice them. And they grew their hair long, probably to look fiercer in battle. Visitors to Sparta saw men and boys constantly training for warfare. Sparta made itself appear "a workshop of war". Other Greeks thought of this small community with terror.

Treatment of cowards

An especially important image at Sparta was that of the coward. Everyone had to see that a coward's life was unbearable—otherwise many men would have refused to do the dangerous soldiering that Sparta required.

Cowards were called "tremblers". They were forbidden to look happy and were insulted, sneered at and hit in the street. When teams were picked for games, the coward was always left out. The moral was, better to die in battle than to live miserably as a coward.

There is a horrifying story told of the lengths to which the Spartans would go to keep the helots from rebelling against their stern rule. In 425 BC a group of helots risked their lives to help Spartan troops who were trapped on the island of Sphakteria. They swam past enemy ships carrying food for their starving masters. Shortly after this, the Spartans told the helots to choose 2000 of their bravest and best men, to whom they promised to give their freedom.

The chosen helots were overjoyed. They went around the temples of Sparta giving thanks. They drank wine and celebrated.

Not long after this, the Spartans murdered all 2000 of the helots. They had contrived the whole episode in order to find out which helots were the boldest and therefore most likely to have the courage to revolt against them. The helots expressed the deep hatred they felt at this savage action when they said they would like to eat the Spartans raw. Ever after this, they watched carefully for signs of Spartan weakness which would allow them to revolt and gain their freedom.

Country Life

Most Greeks lived in the countryside, or very close to it. They did not idealize country life or talk about it in flowery language; they knew too much about the hard work involved to do that.

A poem by Hesiod about country life is still fun to read. It is called *Works and Days* and all the quotations in this section are taken from it. Although it was composed in the 700s BC, many of its details probably applied to the Classical period as well—country life changed slowly.

Hesiod lived in a farming district called Boiotia in central Greece. He tells us that he lived in "a wretched village, Askra, bad in winter, hard in summer". In much of Greece the soil is hard to work and unproductive. A story was told of Peisistratos, the ruler of Athens. He was in the countryside and was surprised to see a farmer working on land which seemed to consist of nothing but stones. So he asked the man what the land produced. "Only hardship and pain," said the farmer, who did not recognize the ruler, "and I'll have to pay ten per cent of that in tax to Peisistratos." In the story Peisistratos admired the hard-working, outspoken farmer and freed him from all taxation.

On rocky ground, grapes and olives were the main crops, as they still are today. (In the picture, olives are being knocked from the trees with sticks. Merchants have come to sample the oil which has been squeezed from the olives in a press.) Better ground was ploughed with oxen to

grow grain. In *Works and Days* Hesiod recommends that a slave helps with the ploughing:

"Get yourself a woman, and an ox to plough—don't marry a woman, buy one, to follow the plough."

Women did much of the labour on a farm, especially at harvest when many hands were needed.

Countrymen worked hard to keep up with their neighbours, as people do today. Hesiod approved:

"A man is eager to work when he looks at another who is rich, who is prompt in ploughing and sowing, and in making his house nice. Neighbour competes with neighbour in his hurry to gain wealth."

In a poor country, this competitiveness could be very useful. It encouraged each farmer to get the most out of his land. But Hesiod warns successful farmers to beware:

"Don't be cheated by some woman who flaunts herself and says wily things to coax you. What she is after is your barn."

We can see that Hesiod had definite views about women.

There were many craftworkers in the villages. They made such things as farm carts, ploughs, fishing nets and beehives. Out on the hillsides, herdsmen looked after sheep and goats. The milk of both animals was made into cheese. In the intense midday heat of summer, things in the country went quiet. People and animals hardly moved. It was then that lonely herdsmen, drowsing in the shade, thought they saw things—like the shepherd god, Pan, playing on his pipes.

Schools

Education at Athens was very different from school today. Boys from wealthy families learned to play music, and trained first as athletes and then as soldiers. In other words, their schooling does not seem to have been very academic. So it is interesting that many Athenian adults were so good at writing plays, history and philosophy.

Most boys were taught to read and write. They practised on wooden tablets covered with wax. (The Athenian form of paper, papyrus from Egypt, was probably too expensive to be used for many exercises.) Misspelling was very common, even in adults. Today it is often difficult to read what Athenians wrote on their vases because of the many strange spellings.

Boys went to school, girls did not. They stayed at home and learned from their mothers. Most girls probably grew up illiterate. Boys' schooling was often short, lasting only between the ages of seven and eleven. It was not compulsory and fathers had to pay for it. The teachers at school were often slaves, so it would be easy for the boys to look down on them. Their fathers certainly would. This suggests that teaching was not thought to be very difficult, or very important. At Sparta, where the training of boys was considered to be vitally important and to need great skill, the teachers were respected citizens.

Reading practice. A teacher holds up a scroll of papyrus for the boy to read. The man on the right may be the boy's father, checking his progress.

A teacher plays the lyre, to accompany his young pupil who is learning to play the double pipes.

Boys at school learned a lot of poetry by heart. The poems of Homer and Hesiod were the most valued, especially when they contained advice. For example, Hesiod had warned people never to trust anyone: "If you make an agreement with your brother ... call a witness." Even a brother might cheat!

Music was taught partly to help people entertain themselves. All music was live, so many musicians were needed. The lyre and the pipes were favourite instruments. Music was also valued because it controlled moods. Think of parties today and how people change the music in order to change the mood.

At the wrestling school, the *palaistra*, athletic training was intended to make boys brave, strong and competitive. It was a preparation for war. When boys were eighteen they did two years' military training. Once they were twenty they were considered ready to face an enemy on the battlefield.

For clever young men, some of the best teaching was given by visiting professors from other Greek states. They taught the vital art of public speaking and also helped to develop ideas on science, philosophy and human nature.

Thinkers

During the 500s BC, thinkers in Miletos and other parts of the Asia Minor coast began to ask difficult questions. Some of the questions still prove challenging today: "How did the world begin?", "How does the world keep its position in space?", "How did the human species come into being?", "What should we think about religion?".

Philosophers thought for themselves when they tried to answer these questions. Unlike many people of the time, they were not content to accept traditional explanations and stories. Much of their reasoning would not be accepted nowadays, but some of their ideas are interestingly close to those of modern thinkers.

Anaximandros of Miletos believed, like some philosophers today, that time had no beginning or end: it stretched away to infinity in both the past and future. He may also have thought that human beings developed somehow from fish, or creatures like fish. Xenophanes explained how a fossil sea-creature came to be found on dry land. He said that in the past the land had been covered by water.

Xenophanes also made an impressive observation about religions. He noted that the Ethiopians portrayed their gods as being like themselves—"with black skin and snub noses". So did the people of Thrace—their gods had blue-grey eyes and red hair. "And," said Xenophanes, "if horses and cows had hands or could draw, they would portray gods in the image of horses and cows."

After Persia had wrecked the town of Miletos, Athens became the centre of advanced thought. Anaxagoras came there from eastern Greece and taught how eclipses were caused. He himself may have learned this from the Babylonians, whose astronomy was quite sophisticated. Anaxagoras was not popular at Athens. Most Athenians still believed that an eclipse was a sign from the gods.

The Athenian philosopher Sokrates made himself even more unpopular. He used clever questioning to show people that their ideas were really rather shallow. Everyone knew nothing, argued Sokrates. He himself was superior because he *realized* he knew nothing!

Sokrates himself wrote no books. But a disciple of his, Plato, made Sokrates the central figure in

Sokrates was found guilty of false teaching. But for his punishment Sokrates suggested he be given free food, which was actually a great honour. The court took this as an insult and sentenced him to death. Sokrates could have escaped but he chose to stay and drink his poison.

many books of philosophy. The most famous of these is the *Republic*. In this, Plato describes his ideal city which would be governed by philosophers. Plato's Sokrates knew much more than the real Sokrates had done. In fact, Plato was often expressing his own ideas through the character of Sokrates.

From Stageira, a remote Greek town, came Aristotle. He became Plato's pupil and wrote books of lecture notes on many subjects. They are very dry, with few jokes or colourful stories. But they do show that Aristotle was one of the cleverest thinkers of all time.

The Games

The Greeks invented athletic contests and held them in honour of their gods. The Isthmian games were staged every two years at the Isthmos of Corinth. The Pythian games took place every four years near Delphi. But the most famous games were those at Olympia, a town in south-western Greece. These also took place every four years and it was in imitation of them that the modern Olympics were started in 1896. The modern games were intended to revive noble Greek practices of old. But in fact some of the Greek practices and motives were not at all noble. There were often ugly scenes—as in today's Olympics.

The Olympic games

The ancient Olympics seem to have begun in the early 700s BC, in honour of Zeus. They were open to athletes from all Greek cities, near and far. Many competitors, for example, came from Sicily and Italy. But foreigners were not allowed to compete. And women were forbidden even to watch. One reason for this was that athletes competed naked. There was a story that one woman was so eager to see her son take part that she joined the spectators disguised as a man. When her son won, she leaped up in excitement and men saw through her disguise. But, if the story is true, she had already seen what she had come to see!

Starting line in the stadium at Olympia. The grooves in the stones gave runners a better grip for their feet.

Events

As in today's Olympics, some events carried more prestige than others. The most respected of all was the foot-race over one length of the stadium— about 200 metres. The winner of this was more honoured than, for example, the victor in the mule-cart race.

There were also contests in jumping, throwing the javelin and discus, chariot-racing, running in hoplite armour, wrestling, boxing, and a ferocious form of brawling known as the *pankration* (see page 71). In this, grappling and punching were allowed. Opponents were not supposed to gouge each other's eyes or to bite, but of course they did.

Perhaps the most serious foul was to bribe the referee. An athlete caught cheating had to pay for a bronze statue of Zeus. This was very expensive, so it served as a fine as well as a way of apologizing to Zeus for defiling his festival. The statues were looted long ago for their metal, but their stone bases can still be seen at Olympia today.

The importance of the Olympics

Even warfare stopped to allow the games to take place. Great crowds gathered. Greeks said that some came to the games to compete, some to

A Greek athlete competes in the long-jump. Unlike modern long-jumpers, he carries a weight in each hand.

watch—and some to buy and sell. So the commercialism of today's Olympics is nothing new, except that Greek traders sold wine and fruit rather than soft drinks and hamburgers.

Victorious athletes received only a token prize, a crown of leaves. Yet they trained hard for months before the games and ate a special diet. Why were the games taken so seriously?

Part of the answer is that several of the events were connected with war. Javelins, chariots and hoplite armour had been, or still were, military equipment. Boxing and wrestling were highly aggressive. So the games were a test of manliness. Also, victory often suggested that the winner had high social status; only the rich could afford to provide champion racehorses or to eat expensive diets and spend their time training.

Successful athletes were treated as heroes in their own communities. One Greek wrote: "They seem fine fellows, and strut about, the darlings of the town." As well as being enjoyable in itself, this no doubt brought the athletes money and other rewards. Perikles' nephew, Alkibiades of Athens, won the chariot-race at Olympia. Because of this victory, Alkibiades said, Athens seemed richer and more powerful than before. So, for a Greek city, victory in the Olympics was a way to suggest military strength. Are the Olympics still used like this today?

Two athletes box (left). Two others grapple in the pankration. *One of them is fouling, by gouging the other's eyes. The referee (right) uses his stick to stop the fouling.*

Model of the sanctuary and games arenas at Olympia. The large building to the left is the temple of Zeus. On the far side is a tunnel leading to the athletics stadium. On the near side is the horse-track and stadium.

Classical Gods and Goddesses

Divine justice

Hesiod, the poet from the little village of Askra, influenced the religion of many later Greeks. He hated aristocratic judges and the way they accepted bribes. So Hesiod wrote that a god, Zeus, would put things to rights. Most Greeks living in the Classical period seem to have agreed with Hesiod. They believed that gods and goddesses punished or rewarded the living.

Zeus, for example, was thought to strike the guilty, especially on voyages and military campaigns. One man, on trial at Athens for murder,

A woman yells in the pain of childbirth. Many died in labour as medical care was primitive. The goddess Artemis (top right) was said to cause these deaths, shooting women with her arrows.

claimed he could not be guilty because he had not been shipwrecked on a recent voyage. The Athenian jury was supposed to believe that punishment from Zeus was reliable.

Mysteries explained

People could not bear to think they did not understand dramatic and important events. They did not understand thunder, so they said it was caused by the anger of Zeus. They believed lightning struck the guilty; eclipses were a sign from heaven and Apollo was responsible for plague. The deaths of women in childbirth were thought to be the work of Apollo's sister, Artemis.

Their beliefs enabled Greeks not to feel helpless. They would sacrifice to a god, giving an animal or wine or treasure, and then feel more confident that evil would pass. Sacrifices were often made on strict condition: "I will give you such-and-such if you answer my prayer." After all, gods were largely modelled on human beings and humans were certainly influenced by gifts. (Even today people sometimes promise to light candles in honour of a saint—if their prayers are answered.)

When archaeologists excavate temples of Asklepios, the Greek god of healing, they find many little clay models—of hands and feet, for example. Grateful worshippers gave these to show which part of the body had been healed.

Seeing into the future

Gods and goddesses knew the past and future. At Delphi, visitors from all over Greece would ask the priestess of Apollo to prophesy for them. Her forecasts were taken very seriously. During the great Persian invasion, she suggested that Athens would be captured and that only a "wooden wall" would survive. This encouraged most Athenians to abandon their city and to fight in their wooden ships. Delphic prophecy, like astrology today, was often designed to have several different meanings. So, if the Athenian fleet had been defeated, the priestess could have claimed that a different wooden wall had been meant.

At another shrine, Dodone, archaeologists have found questions scratched on lead. People asked about their private affairs:

"Shall I become a fisherman?"

"Gerioton asks Zeus whether he should marry."

"Did Dorkilos steal the cloth?"

The temple of Apollo at Delphi, sited to give a dramatic view for the god to enjoy. Before deciding big questions, such as whether to go to war, Greeks often came here to ask Apollo's advice.

"Lysanias asks Zeus and Dione whether the child with whom Annyla is pregnant is his."

In many ways the Greeks were such a clever people that we may be puzzled by their religious beliefs. How could they believe that prophecy worked, that good and evil got their deserts and that gods answered prayers? Part of the answer may be this. *Some* prophecies would prove right, *some* evil people would come to grief and *some* prayers would be followed by success. When this happened, people who wanted their religion to be true would notice eagerly. But when their religion had not proved helpful, they would not be so keen to remember.

Even today, intelligent people often act like this. For example, people usually choose a newspaper which gives a version of the news which supports their political opinions. They are not so keen to read accounts which disprove their ideas.

Religious Festivals

Religious festivals were times for worship, for fun, and sometimes for even stronger excitement. People wore their best clothes. The gods liked to see that mortals were making an effort to please them! And the fine clothes were also a way of showing off to the neighbours.

For women of wealthy family, a festival was one of the few occasions on which it was permitted to be seen in public. So these women took the chance to wear their best jewellery. Necklaces and earrings of gold were meant to show that a woman was not only rich but respectable. At Athens any woman who had been found unfaithful to her husband was forbidden to wear them. Athenian girls from respected families were chosen to carry sacred objects in religious processions. And there was a festival called the Thesmophoria which was especially for women and organized by them.

Getting clothes and make-up ready for the festival was probably part of the fun, like preparing nowadays for a big night out. There was a joke about the famously rich Greek city of Sybaris. Sybarite women, it was said, were told the date of the festival a year in advance. They needed all that time for their fancy preparations.

Rich men at festivals could show off their clothes, sometimes their chariots and above all their precious horses. For poor people, festivals often meant the chance of good "free" food. On most days ordinary citizens could not afford meat. But at festivals cows and sheep were sacrificed, and the meat shared out among the people. One man, who disapproved of *demokratia*, complained that the Athenians had far too many festivals. The poor had used their power to get as many treats as possible!

Different Greek communities had their own forms of festival. Spartans, who specially admired male nudity, held the *gymnopaidiai*, the festival of naked boys. Choruses of boys and young men danced and sang in honour of Apollo. The Olympic games, held in the state of Elis, were sacred to Zeus, as we have seen on pages 70–71. The tragic and comic drama, for which Athens is famous, was performed during festivals in honour of Dionysos. He was the god of "wet nature", as one Greek put it. This meant the powerful natural fluids, such as sap, semen, wine, blood and milk.

In the mountains west of Athens, Greeks worshipped Dionysos in an exciting and mysterious way. Women went out into the countryside to honour the god, and became ecstatic. They wandered for miles, climbing mountains in winter, with an amazing energy. They may also have seen strange visions. People today sometimes have similar experiences after taking certain drugs, and perhaps the Greek women were chemically in-

fluenced in some way. The Athenian playwright, Euripides, wrote of a mythical woman who took part in Dionysos' mountain dance. In a frenzy, she and other women caught and tore apart a young man—her own son—believing him to be a wild animal.

How were festivals thought to please the gods? We have already seen that the gods were imagined as having many human qualities. Gods, like human rulers, would enjoy the praise they received at festivals. Athena would like the fine new robe which, every four years, was put on her most holy statue near the Parthenon. The picture below shows the procession which accompanied the robe up the Akropolis, the cattle to be sacrificed, and vessels containing water and sacrificial wine.

When wine was poured onto the ground, Poseidon—the great god of earthquakes—might drink it. But how did gods and goddesses benefit from the sacrificial meat which people ate? The Greeks had a convenient answer. The immortals enjoyed all the elements of the sacrifice which human beings did not: the fat, the bones, and the smell of the cooking!

Above: A mainad ("raver")—a woman follower of the god Dionysos. Inspired by the god, she can tame nature. She controls a snake and has killed a panther.

Greek Drama

Drama was invented at Athens. It seems to have begun as a group of singers, the chorus, chanting to honour the god Dionysos. Then an actor emerged. A second actor was added by the playwright Aiskhylos, and a third by his younger rival, Sophokles.

There were never more than three actors in each play to take the various speaking roles. Different masks were worn for the different characters—serious-looking for tragedy, frivolous for comedy. All roles, including the many female ones, were played by male actors. No violence was shown on stage.

In spite of these artificial features, audiences were caught up in the action. Aristotle says that tragedy made them feel pity and terror. The plots were usually from legend, and often involved dreadful sufferings.

Oidipous the Tyrant, a play by Sophokles, told how, as a baby, Oidipous was put out to die on a mountain near Thebes. A prophecy had warned that he would grow up to do terrible things.

An actor wearing highly decorated stage boots. He carries a sword and is shown holding a mask, probably to play the character of a king.

Rescued, he returned to Thebes as a young man, killing an older man who had insulted him on the road. He then did the city a great favour, and was made its ruler. He married the widow of the previous ruler and had children by her. The play shows Oidipous as he realizes, years later, that the man he killed was his father, and the woman he married is his mother. This means that his children are also his brothers and sisters. In horror, the wife-and-mother kills herself. Oidipous, taking a brooch from her dress, puts out his own eyes. He then comes in front of the audience, a blinded and broken figure, with his wretched children.

The central figure in a tragedy was usually, like Oidipous, of mixed character. The Athenians were sophisticated people: they did not want to see total villains, oozing malice, because in real life such characters rarely exist. The tragic figure was usually good enough for the audience to pity him, and bad enough for them not to feel that his fate was an outrage.

The great figures of tragedy were rulers and aristocrats. But the audiences were made up mainly of ordinary, fairly poor, people. We can tell this from the size of the theatre at Athens. It held over 10,000—many more even than the assembly. Ordinary citizens often resented the wealthy aristocrats. Perhaps one reason why Athenians so enjoyed tragedy was that it showed aristocrats *suffering*. In the theatre the poor could look down on, feel pity for, the rich.

The picture on the opposite page shows a scene from a tragedy. Two characters act out the drama while the chorus comments on the action.

Comedy was much more relaxed, with jokes about daily life, politics and sex. Again, the rich and famous were the targets of criticism, but this time they were real people—the politicians and celebrities of Athens. Perikles was teased about being under the thumb of his girlfriend, Aspasia. The tragedian Euripides was mocked for supposedly being the son of a greengrocer. (This shows that Athenians could be snobs.)

Aristophanes, perhaps the greatest comic poet, disapproved of the war against Sparta (the Peloponnesian war). He showed a character travelling to heaven to beg Zeus for peace—riding on a dung-beetle. In his play *Lysistrate* he shows the women of Greece trying to end the war. So long as the fighting goes on they refuse to make love to their husbands. This quickly stops the war!

The Peloponnesian war

The Spartans had long dreaded the growing power of Athens. With their great navy, the Athenians might one day intervene in Sparta's own affairs and wreck its economy by causing the helots to revolt. So Athens had to be conquered. But Sparta's citizen warriors numbered fewer than 4000; Athens had far more—perhaps ten times as many. So the Spartans used a cunning strategy: they decided only to begin a war when Athens was in difficulties.

In 431 BC a chance came. Much of Athens' army was away, dealing with rebels in the empire. Sparta invaded Athens' homeland, using its strongest weapon—the phalanx of hoplites, made up of Spartans and allies from the Peloponnese. But the Athenians, advised by Perikles, refused to give battle. Instead they used their own greatest strength, the navy, to bring in food and money from the empire. Sparta's own fleet was too small to interfere. There was a stalemate. The Spartans dominated on land in southern and central

A coin of the island state of Aigina, showing its symbol—a turtle. In the 500s BC the men of Aigina were great traders. But in nearby Athens, independent, unfriendly Aigina was called "the eyesore of the Peiraieus". Athens conquered it in the 450s BC, and added it to the Athenian empire.

The allies of Athens, controlled by Athens' navy, lay mostly out of reach of Sparta's land army. This dominated most of southern and central Greece.

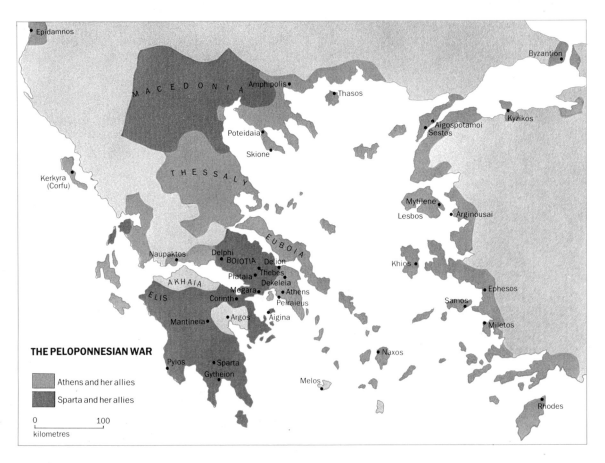

THE PELOPONNESIAN WAR

☐ Athens and her allies

☐ Sparta and her allies

0 — 100
kilometres

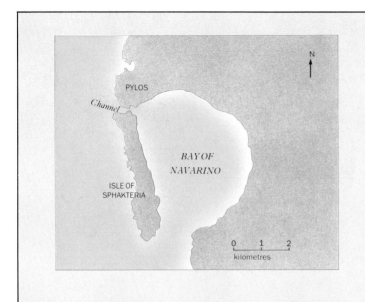

This map shows the position of the isle of Sphakteria, part of Sparta's territory of Messenia. In 425 BC the Athenians used their navy to seize the headland of Pylos. So Sparta placed a few hundred men on the island itself. But Athenian ships cut them off, then landed a large force. The Athenians burned the woods in which the Spartans were hiding, shot arrows and stones through the smoke, and surrounded the survivors. The Spartans surrendered—something they were never supposed to do. Athens was elated.

Greece. Athenian ships controlled the islands, and the coasts north and east of the Aegean.

Then, in 425 BC, Athens captured about 120 Spartans on the island of Sphakteria (see above). This was a sizeable fraction of Sparta's small population. They became hostages and Sparta had to stop raiding Athens' homeland. Instead, it sent a land army of desperadoes to the north of the Aegean. Once there, it captured important Athenian possessions. To get these back, Athens agreed to give up its hostages. On that basis, peace was made in 421 BC.

Between 415 and 413 BC Athens tried to capture Sicily. Two great Athenian fleets, carrying about 40,000 men, bore down on the main Sicilian city of Syracuse, and nearly captured it. Victory would have made Athens ruler of the Mediterranean. But mistakes, and the arrival at Syracuse of a Spartan force, tipped the balance. In 413, the whole of Athens' great force was trapped and annihilated.

Athens' troubles in Sicily gave Sparta another great chance. It re-opened war in Greece, obtained money from Persia and built a large fleet. Athens' empire began to crumble as rich men in the subject states saw their chance to throw off Athenian rule, and the *demokratia* that went with it. Sparta's fleet captured the Athenian navy by a clever trick (405 BC), then cut off the grain ships by which Athens was fed. The Athenians starved, and surrendered in 404. The Spartans took over their empire.

A common, sad, scene. A husband waves goodbye as he leaves for war. His wife offers him and his fellow-warrior a libation.

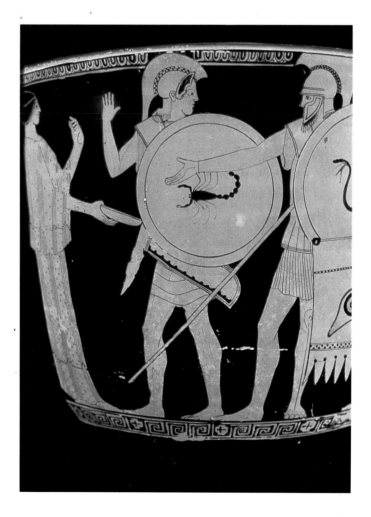

Sparta and Macedon

Sparta

When Sparta conquered Athens in 404 BC, rich men rejoiced. They said that the day of freedom for Greece had at last arrived. The Spartans demolished the long walls between Athens and its port, Peiraieus—the walls which for half a century had prevented Sparta from encircling and cutting off the Athenians. Flute girls were hired to play while the walls fell. They were favourite entertainers at rich men's parties and now the rich were celebrating. In Athens' former empire the Spartans and their wealthy supporters carried out massacres of democrats. Governments favourable to Sparta were set up.

Sparta's rule over Greece was not well conducted. Spartan officials quarrelled with one another, and undid each other's work. Even

Greece in the 300s BC. After the fall of Sparta's empire, Philip of Macedon expanded first eastwards then through Thessaly into the heart of Greece.

Sparta's supporters were offended when, in 382 BC, a Spartan army seized control of the city of Thebes in peacetime and without an excuse. There was also a clumsy attempt by a Spartan commander to seize Peiraieus, again in peacetime. The Spartans had called themselves the champions of freedom, but now they seemed to be its enemy.

Sparta also suffered from a shortage of population. Its armies abroad were often too small; several little forces were overwhelmed by more numerous enemies. In the process many Spartan commanders were killed, including the cunning Lysandros (Lysander) who, in 405 BC, had captured Athens' navy. It was shortage of men which caused Sparta to do a remarkable thing for a Greek state. It allowed women to make some of the important public decisions.

In the early 300s BC Athens regained her independence, and even went to war against Sparta once more. The Athenians tried to rebuild an empire, but this time their allies were wary of them. In Athens itself the old enthusiasm had gone. Many Athenians probably felt they were

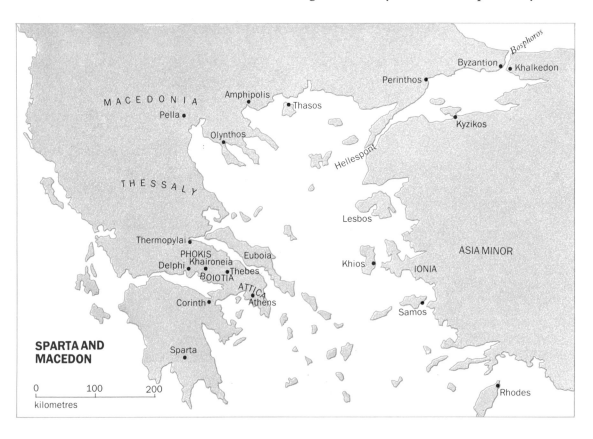

SPARTA AND MACEDON

0 — 100 — 200
kilometres

lucky that Sparta had not demolished the whole city in 404 BC. If they were to build another threatening empire, and be beaten again by Sparta, they could expect no mercy.

Thebes

Thebes grew in power. After throwing off Spartan rule, Theban troops used their numbers to crush the long-dreaded but now very small Spartan army. At Leuktra (near Thebes) a phalanx of Thebans, 50 lines deep, surged into the Spartan lines (371 BC). It killed a large number of Sparta's remaining citizens. Not long afterwards, the Thebans invaded Sparta's homeland. The helots at last had the protection they needed to stage a successful revolt. Sparta lost the great helot territory of Messenia—for ever, as it turned out.

Sparta's citizen soldiers now numbered fewer than 1000. They had lost their reputation, both for being invincible and for behaving honourably. Sparta's days as a great power were over.

The glory of Thebes was short-lived, however. Hostile neighbours of Thebes, the Phocians, seized the great shrine at Delphi. They melted down the treasure of gold and silver which Greek states over centuries had put there to honour Apollo. This melted treasure was then turned by the Phocians into coins. And the coins bought the Phocians a great army of mercenary soldiers from many parts of Greece.

This army and the army of Thebes wore each other down during the 350s BC. During the same period, Athens nearly went bankrupt as it tried in vain to hold on to a little empire. Greece was exhausted. And an enemy on its north-eastern border was well placed to take advantage of this weakness. The enemy was Macedon and its ruler, King Philip. The Macedonians were not fully Greek but they had many Greek characteristics.

Philip of Macedon

Philip owned a goldmine. He used part of his wealth to buy support in Greek states. He also built up a mercenary army of his own, and gave his troops more practice than most Greek hoplites ever got. He led his men with energy and courage. When besieging one Greek state, he was hit by an arrow and lost an eye. But he went on with the siege until victory.

An ivory head, found recently at Vergina in Macedonia. It comes from a tomb which was probably that of Philip, and it seems to show the king himself. Philip was blinded in one eye. Notice the groove through the eyebrow (left).

In the winter of 339–8 BC Philip took perhaps his biggest risk. He marched into central Greece and challenged the combined armies of Thebes and Athens. At the battle of Khaironeia, in 338 BC, he won. He treated Athens leniently. He may well have wanted the Athenian navy to help him in a great campaign he planned in the east. But he did not live to carry out this plan.

In 336 BC, at home in Macedonia, Philip was murdered. It was left to his son to take on his scheme. The son was a young man named Alexander.

Alexander the Great

When Philip was murdered, the outlook for his kingdom of Macedonia was bleak. He left great debts. And the new king, his son Alexander, was only twenty. He was so small that his enemies called him "just a boy". But he had a scheme.

Alexander borrowed even more money, to finance a huge army of conquest. He planned to use it to capture the Persian empire, and so to pay off all his debts. A simple scheme, and hair-raising. It looked truly childish. Was it?

Persia's territory was vast, as we have seen (page 48). From the point of view of people in Greece and Macedonia, the Persian empire stretched even further to the east than the Mediterranean Sea did to the west. And it had to be crossed on foot, a slow form of travel compared with sailing in a trireme. In practical terms, Persia's eastern provinces were much further away than the furthest Greek colonies in Gaul and Spain. Alexander would be leading his men into a new world.

Unknown territory to the east

Most Greeks did not *want* to be led into a new world, if that meant going far inland. Soldiers of an earlier Greek army, which had crossed Asia Minor, shouted with relief when at last they saw "The sea! The sea!". Once at the sea, Greeks felt they could always get home. But would an army follow Alexander so far from the sea that getting home seemed an impossible dream?

Alexander could reason as follows: the hoplite phalanx of the Greeks had regularly managed to beat the lighter-armed foot-soldiers of the Persians. But the Greek states, jealous of each other, had never united to invade the Persian empire. Now, for the first time, Macedonia and Greece were dominated by one man—himself. He had a unique chance to see what a colossal phalanx could do—provided the men would follow him.

In 334 BC Alexander invaded Asia Minor. The war was on. The main body of his army seems to have been made up of about 12,000 Macedonians and the same number of Greeks. They fought in heavy armour, with pikes about four metres long.

In his first victory over the Persians, at the river Granikos, Alexander showed how he would keep

The head of Alexander the Great on a coin.

his men loyal. He fought with obvious bravery—commanding from the front, a position of danger. He even wore a pair of white wings on his helmet, which meant that the enemy could easily identify and attack him. Later in his campaign he went first up a siege ladder into an enemy fortress. His officers begged him afterwards never to risk his life like that again. But his bravery won him deep respect from the ordinary soldiers. He was a commander they would follow almost anywhere.

In the next year (333 BC) the Persian king, Darius III, tackled Alexander himself. At the battle of Issos, Darius was defeated trying to prevent the invaders from entering Syria. In 331 came the greatest battle of all, at the heart of the empire. Alexander's force was greatly outnumbered but it was well disciplined. It overcame Darius' host and war-chariots, on the plain of Gaugamela. Soon after, Darius was murdered by his own men.

Alexander had won the Persian empire. But he did not rest. He pressed on to the east. He was heading for the end of the world.

The world was thought to end at the eastern coast of India. To reach it, Alexander fought the brave king Poros—and his terrifying war elephants—in the Punjab (326 BC). The animals trampled many of Alexander's men, and sheltered Poros's own troops. By attacking from the rear,

CLASSICAL GREECE

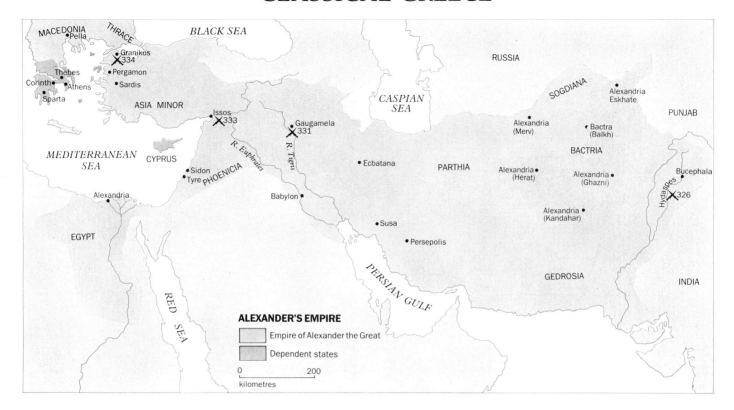

ALEXANDER'S EMPIRE

Empire of Alexander the Great

Dependent states

0   200
kilometres

away from the animals, Alexander managed to win. But his men had had enough. They had heard that going further into India would mean crossing a desert, and facing far greater numbers of enemy elephants. They refused to go on.

Alexander sulked, and pretended he would go on without them. But, of course, he could not. To a great cheer from the army, it was announced that they were turning back.

Alexander's empire

Alexander wanted to do more than just conquer. He wanted his empire to last. To guard against revolts and invasions, he founded many colonies in the Greek style, populated by his former soldiers. Many were called "Alexandria". The most important of these was to be the Alexandria which protected and governed Egypt.

Alexander knew there would be trouble if his little garrisons were hated by their subjects and the former ruling class of Persia. So he treated the Persians with respect. He arranged for thousands of his men to marry Persian women. There was some resistance to this; Greeks had long despised Persians as slavish barbarians. But Alexander himself married an eastern woman, Roxane from Bactria. He was doing what he had done so successfully before—leading by example.

An Indian painting in which Alexander is supervising the building of a defensive wall (of fire). The scene, painted over 1000 years after Alexander's time, shows the lasting reputation of this man who conquered much of north-western India.

The Hellenistic World

Alexander died young, in 323. His empire broke into pieces. His former generals and friends fought each other for control. His young widow, Roxane, was murdered. The son she had borne him was also killed. If allowed to grow up he would have been an unbearable threat to the generals.

The struggle to control Macedonia and Greece went on for many years. But these lands were no longer seen as the main prize. Their wealth was almost trivial when compared to that of the new territories in Asia and Egypt.

The conquered areas of Asia, most of Alexander's former empire, were secured by Seleukos, who had served Alexander as a general. His family kept an empire, though a shrinking one, for about two-and-a-half centuries. Egypt, smaller but easy to protect and hugely rich, passed to another former general, Ptolemy. He, and his family after him, ruled for almost three centuries.

Because of Alexander's conquests, there was now a large area of the world in which the ruling and educated classes spoke Greek and followed Greek customs. The Greek word for "Greece" was *Hellas*. The civilization which Alexander founded is known as *Hellenistic*.

Alexandria

After gaining Egypt, Ptolemy stole the embalmed corpse of Alexander. He took it to his capital, Alexandria, and put it on show. He did this to advertise his claim that the kingdom of Egypt was the main heir to Alexander's glory. Ptolemy's claim turned out to be justified. Alexandria became the chief city of the Greek-speaking world.

It has been said that two great rivers ran through Egypt. One was the Nile; the other was a river of grain, flowing down into the granaries of Alexandria. It was the peasant workers of Egypt who supplied this wealth for their new masters, and made it possible for the Ptolemies to put their great scheme into action. This was to hire and develop the best brains of the Greek world.

The *Mouseion*—the first museum—was set up in Alexandria. It was a research institute, and scholars working there received generous salaries. To help their work, a library was founded. It was said to have a copy of every important work in the Greek language. The books took the form of scrolls of Egyptian papyrus. (When a rival library was founded at Pergamon in Asia Minor, the authorities in Egypt refused to let it have papyrus. Instead its books were written on animal skin—*pergamene*, from which we get the word "parchment".)

The thinkers of Alexandria had different interests from those of Archaic and Classical Greece.

Petra in Jordan: Greek architecture in a very un-Greek setting. Columns have been carved into the living rock.

THE HELLENISTIC WORLD

Eastern Greeks and Athenians had speculated about religion and politics. But now Hellenistic rulers were themselves worshipped as gods. Anyone who speculated about *their* status, or who suggested a different political system, might get into serious trouble. One writer was crucified for saying that Hellenistic rulers' purple robes looked like the purple wounds on a whipped slave. Another was drowned for writing a rude poem about the marriage of a Ptolemy. Writers learned to look for safer subjects.

Scholarship, science and maths

Sentimental poetry became fashionable. In the crowded and dirty streets of Alexandria, people liked to hear about a cleaner, more peaceful, way of life. So they enjoyed Theokritos' new poems about life in the countryside. These told of happy, leisured shepherds playing music and courting shepherdesses.

Scholarship was another safe pursuit for writers. Some of the great literature of the Greek past was now found difficult to understand, and needed explaining. So, using the library at Alexandria, men wrote commentaries on the texts of the past.

Hellenistic thinkers had their greatest success with mathematics and science. Euclid's work was of such a high standard that geometry was called "Euclid" until the 20th century. The old theories of Arkhimedes of Syracuse still earn the respect of

A doctor uses the new medical knowledge to examine his patient, a small boy.

mathematicians today. He was also known for his war machines. He designed a crane which, based on land, grabbed and tipped up enemy ships attacking his city. He is said also to have used mirrors to set ships on fire, by concentrating the sun's rays.

Eratosthenes used geometry to calculate the circumference of the earth, coming very close to the true figure. Aristarkhos, unlike most scientists of the day, argued that the earth went round the sun and not *vice versa*.

Doctors made discoveries about the body. Human corpses were held to be sacred; if they were cut up, their owners might have trouble in the life after death. So scientists dissected the corpses of monkeys instead, and learned about the human body in that way.

Hellenistic engineers knew about cogwheels and gears. They could also build simple steam engines. But there was no industrial revolution.

An ancient Greek slot machine. The coin, falling onto a plate, lifts a lever and releases water—for use in a temple.

Decline and Renewal

The Seleukid rulers, who inherited Alexander's conquests in Asia, struggled to prevent their empire from crumbling. Alexander's plan to unite the empire by marriage had failed. Most of the Greeks and Macedonians who had married Persian women divorced them as soon as Alexander died. Many of the soldiers were reluctant to stay in the remote eastern provinces to guard the frontiers. When Alexander died, they tried to march westwards and home. Seleukos willingly gave up territory in India, however. He exchanged it for 500 Indian war elephants—a hugely powerful weapon which would help him protect his remaining lands.

By frightening enemies, these animals did prolong Seleukid rule. But even so, new Greek-ruled kingdoms were set up in territory once controlled by the Seleukids. These kingdoms were vigorous and independent, such as Bactria in the east, and Pergamon to the west in Asia Minor.

The Hellenistic world might have lasted far longer if it had done more to exploit its technology. Arkhimedes' war machines held up Rome's conquest of Syracuse in Sicily for a time, but many inventions were used only as toys. Industrial production was despised as slaves' work.

The rise of Rome
Gradually the shadow of Rome fell over the Hellenistic kingdoms of the eastern Mediterranean. On Roman orders, the Seleukids crippled their war elephants in 163 BC. Greece itself was finally conquered by Rome in 146 BC. In 133 the king of Pergamon left his territory to Rome in his will. In the 60s BC Rome extinguished the last power of the Seleukids in Syria. By the 40s there was only one great kingdom left. This was Egypt, and it was ruled by the famous Cleopatra VII, "the Queen of Kings".

Cleopatra cunningly tried to retain her power by becoming the lover of leading Romans—first of Julius Caesar, then of Mark Antony. Through her influence over Antony she even managed for a time to dominate parts of the Roman empire, in Syria and Asia Minor. But Octavian, who was later to become the emperor Augustus, overcame her forces and Antony's in 31 BC. Rome, it seemed, had finally won.

But the Romans had already fallen under the Greek spell. They copied Greek styles of building, of writing in prose and verse, and of philosophy. The emperor Augustus disapproved of this Greek influence and emphasized the Italian elements in Roman life. But when his finest poet, Vergil, wrote a great work in his honour—the *Aeneid*—it was largely modelled on the Greek poetry of Homer. As another Roman poet said, captive Greece had taken captive its savage captor, Rome. Later emperors came to depend on clever Greeks, exslaves, to help them run their empire.

The rise and fall of Byzantion
In the early 300s AD, Christianity was recognized as a dominant religion of the Roman world. It was

A cunning machine—but for a religious, not an industrial, purpose. Heat from the fire on the altar expands air in the globe. Pressure from the air forces water up a tube and into a bucket, pulling open the temple doors—by a miracle!

DECLINE AND RENEWAL

Jewish in origin but its sacred text, the New Testament, was first written down in Greek. This was the language of educated people in the near east. And it was from the Greek east that Christianity spread to Rome. Constantine, an emperor who converted to Christianity, moved the capital of the Roman empire in AD 330. He moved it to Byzantion, a Greek city, which he then renamed Constantinople. Its inhabitants were proud to call themselves "Romans", but they did not speak Latin, the language of Rome. These new Romans spoke Greek.

In the 400s AD, barbarian invaders conquered the western Roman empire. In the 600s, the Romans in the east (now known as Byzantines) lost the southern provinces of Egypt and Syria to Muslim Arabs. But it was not until 1453 that Muslim Turks fought their way through the walls of Constantinople itself, and captured it.

Many Muslims, and Christians, had despised the culture of ancient Greece because of its pagan religion. Most of the writings of the Greeks were lost for ever. The great library of Alexandria was destroyed in the 200s AD—perhaps the saddest single event in the history of learning. But a few scholars, Arabs and Byzantines, copied out and studied the works of the early Greek writers. Some of their manuscripts were taken to Italy where, in the 1400s, they helped to spread a rebirth of learning about the ancient Greeks and Romans.

The Renaissance

This rebirth of Greek and Roman thought is known as the Renaissance. The thousand years after the fall of the western Roman empire had been a slow time for the development of ideas. To have new ideas and to question Christian beliefs had often been thought wrong. But now people began to turn to the Greeks and Romans for their learning. Some schools taught ancient Greek, so that scholars could find out for themselves what the Greeks had written. Many more read the ancient texts in translation. Dramatists, such as Racine in France and Shakespeare in England, wrote plays which took ideas from the drama and myth of the ancient world.

In the early 1800s, many Greek sculptures were brought to northern Europe. Greek art became the fashion, and Greek ideas retained their importance in the thinking of educated people.

Mosaic from a church in Constantinople. The scene shows the Roman emperor handing a model of the church to the Virgin Mary. Notice the inscription in Greek.

Walls of Constantinople, built by Theodosius in the 5th century AD. Constantinople was a city founded by ancient Greeks and expanded by a Roman emperor. It inherited the eastern Roman empire.

The Ancient Greeks Today

In the last few centuries, people have often liked to look back to a chosen part of the ancient world. During the 19th century, some looked to the world of the Old Testament. They gave their children biblical names, such as Rebecca and Jonah, Hiram and Abigail. In the 1970s a Prime Minister of Britain likened himself to Moses.

Other people preferred to look back to the Roman empire, especially during the 1800s when several European states had empires of their own. Emperors copied the Roman title of "Caesar": in Germany, the Kaiser; in Russia, the Czar. But today it is perhaps ancient Greece to which people most like to look back. Why is this?

A common outlook

One reason is that our civilization likes to be creative, to look for new ideas and not always to follow tradition. The Greeks were also great creators, as we have seen. In today's world people question authority more than they used to. The Greeks did this—it was part of being creative. Today we are often suspicious of empires. There is more respect for community politics in which it is easier for individuals to participate and make their mark. This outlook helps us to appreciate *demokratia* and life in the little *polis*. And lastly, openness is now in fashion. This is perhaps the first time for over 2000 years that society has been

able to accept the bawdy bits in Athenian comedy. All these modern trends help us to enjoy and understand the ancient Greeks.

The Greek language lives on outside Greece

Scientists still show their respect for the Greeks by the language they use. "Energy" and "atom", "symptom" and "syndrome", "electron" and "catalyst" are among thousands of scientific terms of Greek origin. The word-endings -ism, -ise and -ology are from Greek. The American word "astronaut" ("star sailor") is made up of Greek words. So is the Russian word "cosmodrome" ("universe runway"). A popular film about a voyage of adventure through space was called a "space odyssey". Common Greek words such as *poly* (many), *mega* (big) and *micro* (small) are still used, to form not only technical words but also slang ("mega-bucks", "mega-expensive").

Even our alphabet comes from the ancient Greeks—by way of the Romans, who made some changes to the Greek script. (The word "alphabet" is itself made up from the first two Greek letters, *alpha* and *beta*.) The Cyrillic script, which is used in Russian and other east European languages, also came from the Greek alphabet, but by a different route. Look at a Russian stamp. It says CCCP (which is SSSR in our script). The C takes its shape from the Greek letter for S—*sigma* (see below). A Greek poet called the crescent moon, "the great sigma in the sky".

Ideas borrowed from ancient Greece

Today we can still see much of the landscape familiar to the ancient Greeks. Many a coastal

The standard Greek alphabet, which has changed only slightly since Perikles' time. Equivalents are shown in our own "Roman" alphabet, which itself is derived from the Greek.

Capital letter	Α	Β	Γ	Δ	Ε	Ζ	Η	Θ	Ι	Κ	Λ	Μ	Ν	Ξ	Ο	Π	Ρ	Σ	Τ	Υ	Φ	Χ	Ψ	Ω
Small letter	α	β	γ	δ	ε	ζ	η	θ	ι	κ	λ	μ	ν	ξ	ο	π	ρ	σ	τ	υ	φ	χ	ψ	ω
Name of letters	alpha	beta	gamma	delta	epsilon	zeta	eta	theta	iota	kappa	lambda	mu	nu	xi	omikron	pi	rho	sigma	tau	upsilon	phi	khi	psi	omega
Equivalent "Roman" letter	A / a	B / b	G / g	D / d	E (short) / e	Z / z	E (long) / e	Th / th	I / i	K / k	L / l	M / m	N / n	X / x	O (short) / o	P / p	R / r	S / s	T / t	U / u	Ph,F / ph,f	Kh,Ch / kh,ch	Ps / ps	O (long) / o

THE ANCIENT GREEKS TODAY

For thousands of years Greek houses like these have clustered by the sea, on hillsides near a harbour.

town in Greece still clusters round its harbour, with little houses clinging to the side of a hill which once served as a fortress. The temples surviving at Athens are well known, though the crowds of visitors make the Akropolis rather busier than it was in Perikles' time. Some of the finest Greek buildings are in fact in Sicily and southern Italy, where colonists from mainland Greece once grew rich. Coastal Turkey, too, has many interesting Greek ruins, some of them seldom explored.

One of the loveliest remaining buildings is the temple of Aphaia. This is near Athens on the isle of Aigina. The sailors of Aigina traded with distant lands. Standing by the temple today, looking out over the Aegean sea, it is easy to imagine the relief and excitement those returning sailors felt. Shining in the distance on its lonely hilltop, they could see their little shrine. They knew that they were home.

In many cities nowadays we can see buildings made in the Greek style. They remind us of a Greek temple, with a row of tall columns at the entrance. These modern buildings are mostly libraries, churches, government headquarters and theatres. They are places where people go to do what the Greeks are best remembered for—thinking.

Our Olympic games imitate the Greek games, as we have seen. Foreigners and women are, of course, no longer excluded. But the games are still a form of political competition because, as in Greek times, the athletes are seen as representing their states.

In schools and colleges people still study the two subjects which the Greeks invented—history and philosophy. They also study the ancient Greeks themselves, and their language, often specializing in narrow areas such as Mycenaean archaeology, Homeric language, drama, social history or vase painting.

Greek dramas are staged all over the world. This is usually for enjoyment but sometimes there is also a political purpose. If people want to protest against a heavy-handed government, they sometimes stage a Greek play about tyranny. If the government complains, they say: "What's wrong? It's only an old play!" But the "old plays" of the Greeks have ideas which are powerful even today.

A modern athlete (Daley Thompson) completes a long-jump in the Olympic games. Both the event and the games were first thought up by the Greeks.

SPELLING GREEK WORDS

For many years it was usual to write Greek names with the Roman spelling. But today's scholars often prefer to keep closer to the original Greek spellings. That's what we have done in this book. So, we write *ai* instead of *ae*, *oi* instead of *oe*, *os* instead of *us*, *k* instead of *c*. Here are some examples of names, first in the Roman spelling and then in the form closer to the original.

Place names

Acropolis	Akropolis
Aegina	Aigina
Boeotia	Boiotia
Chius	Khios
Euboea	Euboia
Halicarnassus	Halikarnassos
Miletus	Miletos
Mount Olympus	Mount Olympos

Personal names

Herodotus	Herodotos
Lysander	Lysandros
Oedipus	Oidipous
Pericles	Perikles
Sophocles	Sophokles
Themistocles	Themistokles

We have, however, kept the Roman spelling in the case of a few names which are now famous and unalterable: *Phoenicia, Mycenae, Alexander, Plato, Sappho,* and *Thucydides* are examples.

LOOKING FURTHER

If you would like to find out more about the Greeks, there is no shortage of interesting books. First, there are the books which the Greeks themselves wrote. Almost all the most important are well translated in the *Penguin Classics* series. Homer's *Odyssey* makes a good start, an adventure story with elements of the supernatural, set among palaces and beautiful scenery. The *Iliad* is a more narrowly warlike tale. But if you read it, keep a sharp look-out for the many brief glimpses of peaceful Dark Age life. Hesiod's *Works and Days* is a strange and interesting mixture of superstition and practical advice.

Herodotos' *Persian Wars* is far less military than its title suggests. In fact, it is one of the best collections of stories (including tall stories) ever made. Thucydides' *Peloponnesian War* is magnificent, but (unlike Herodotos) it isn't light enough for bedside reading.

Of the great tragic poets, Aiskhylos (Aeschylus), Sophokles and Euripides, perhaps the one most enjoyed today is Euripides. His *Medeia* is a famous treatment of the position of women, and his *Bakkhai* (*Bacchae*) looks at a wild and unfamiliar side of Greek life. The comedies of Aristophanes give the best picture of daily life in the streets and houses of Athens. Many of his jokes are still funny, and some are extremely rude.

As a first step into Greek philosophy, look at the short, dramatic dialogues in *Plato: The Last Days of Socrates* (Penguin 1969) which include the story of Sokrates' trial and execution.

For looking at Greek vase paintings there are two very good books by John Boardman: *Athenian Black Figure Vases* and *Athenian Red Figure Vases* (Thames and Hudson 1974 and 1975). Each has a mass of photographs.

Older students will enjoy John Chadwick's *The Decipherment of Linear B* (Cambridge University Press), the story of a breakthrough in the study of the Mycenaeans. Oswyn Murray's *Early Greece* (Fontana 1980) is a good introduction to the early period. A.R. Burn's *Pelican History of Greece* (Penguin 1970) covers the whole period. For older students, the writer of this book has written *Constructing Greek History* (Croom Helm 1988) which looks in detail at Classical Athens and Sparta.

There are superb collections of Greek objects to be seen in Athens (especially at the National Archaeological Museum), in London (at the British Museum), in New York (at the Metropolitian Museum of Art), and in Paris (at the Louvre).

Best of all, perhaps, there are the ruins of the ancient Greek cities and fortresses. The beauty of their setting in the intense Greek light is something no photograph can prepare you for.

INDEX

Note: page numbers in *italics*
refer to illustrations.